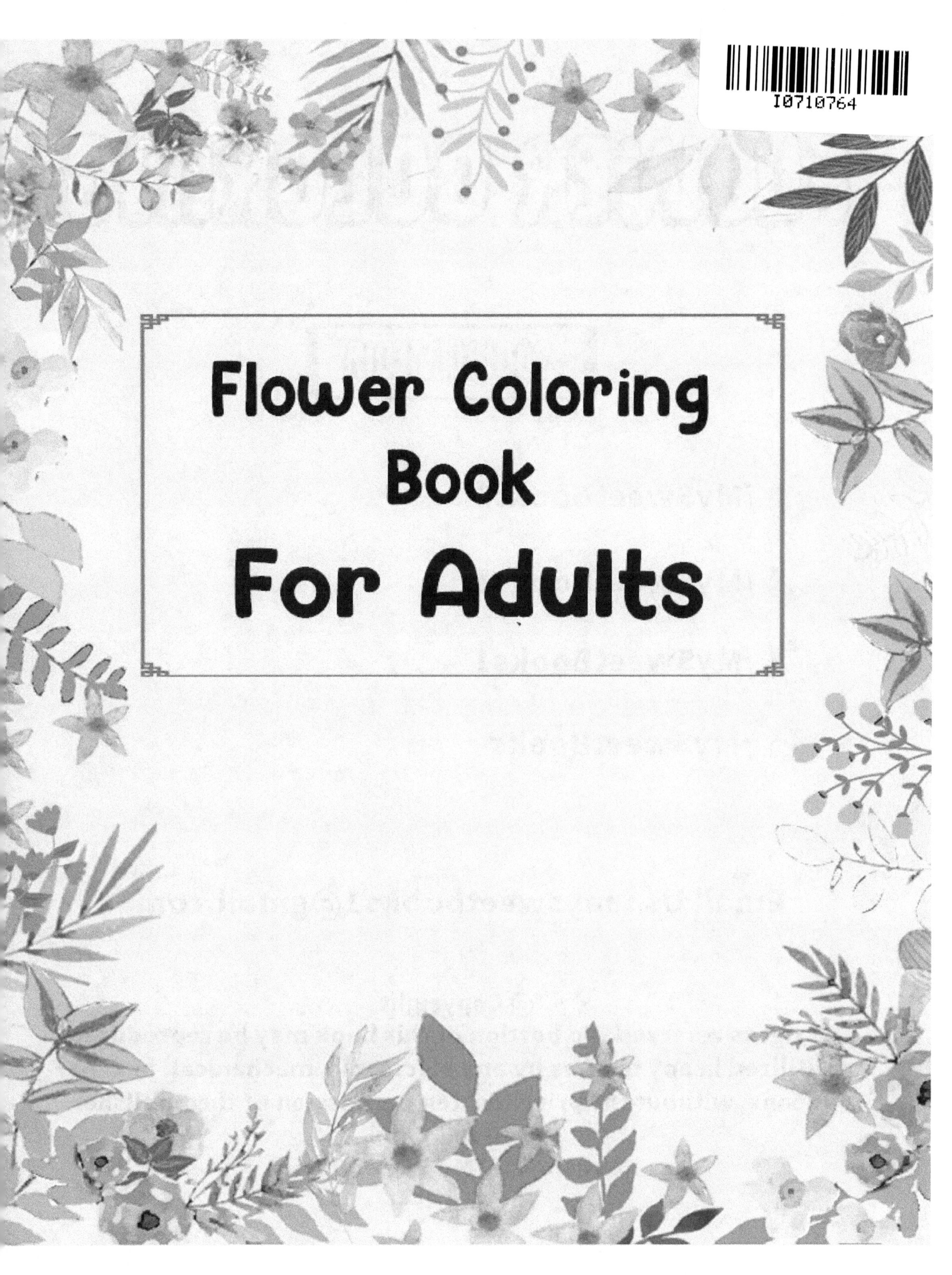

Flower Coloring
Book
For Adults

FLOWER COLORING

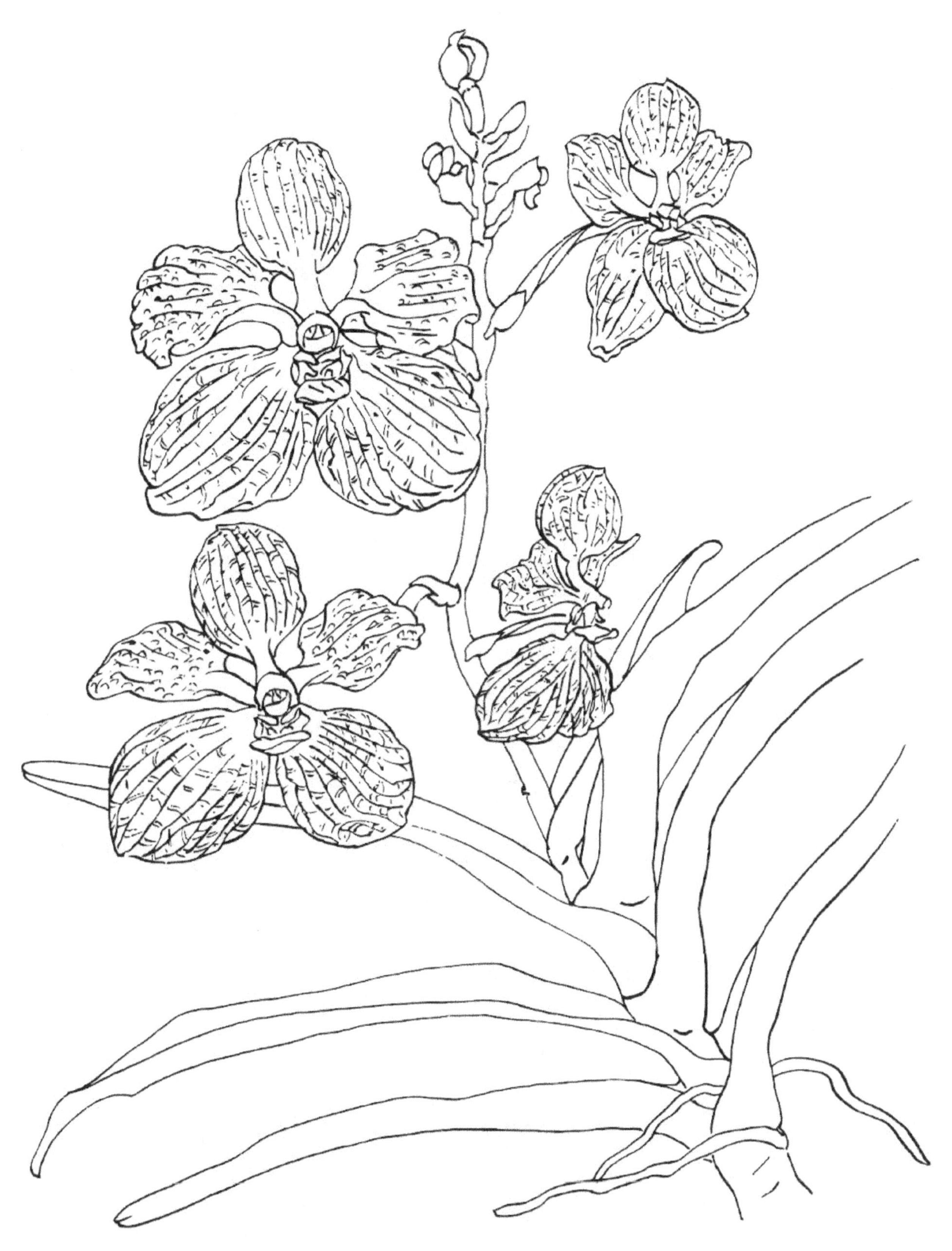

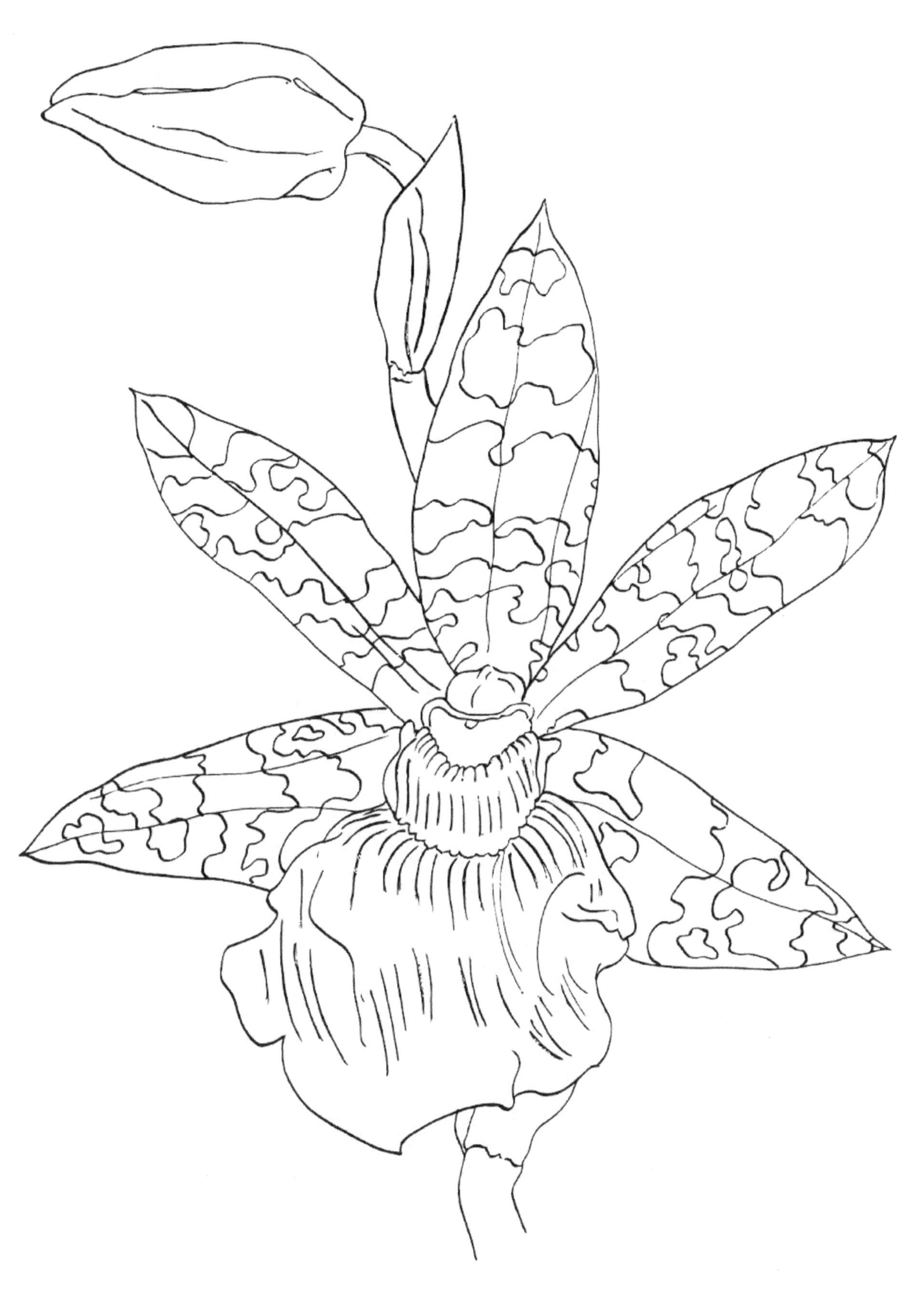

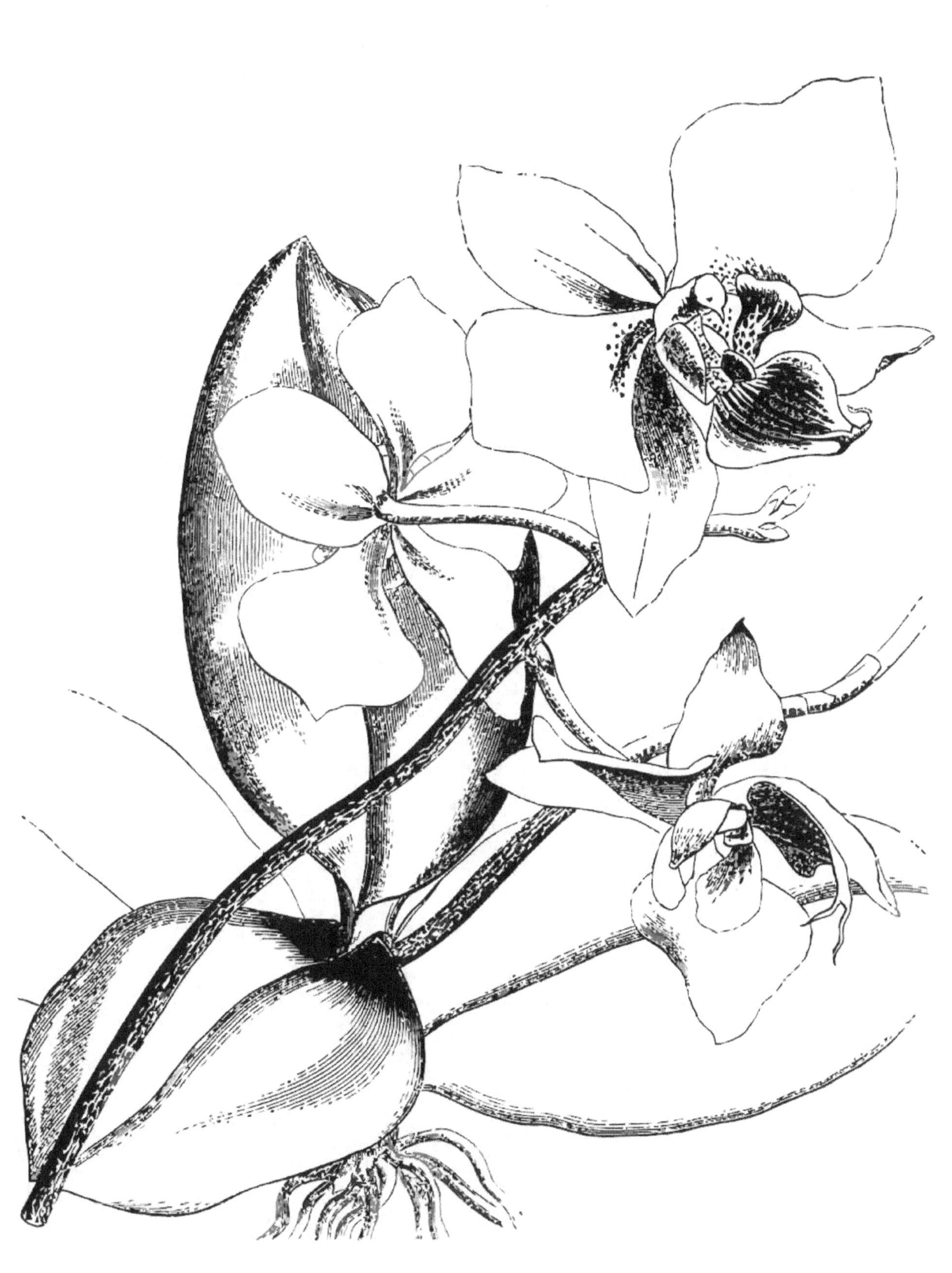

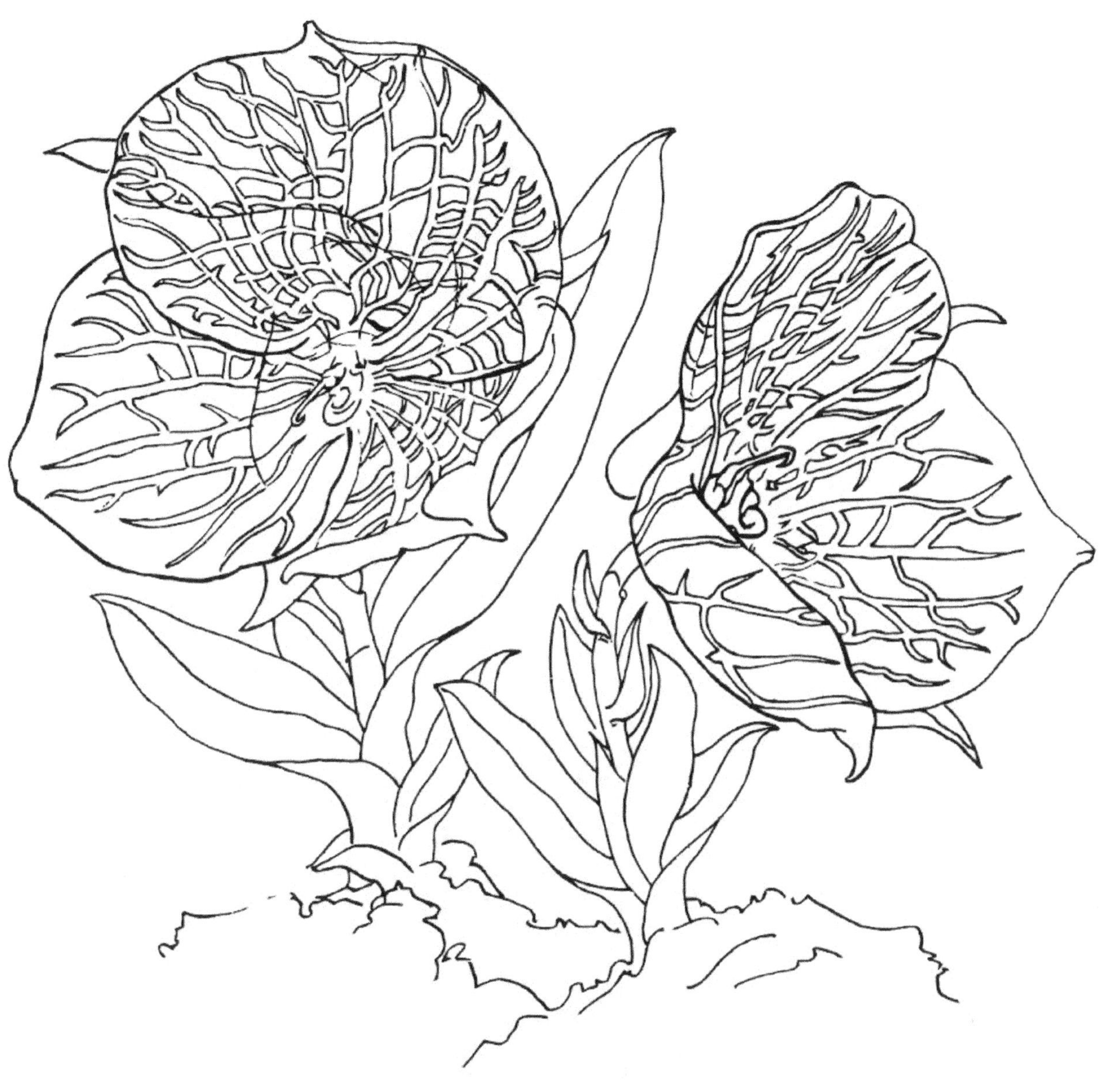

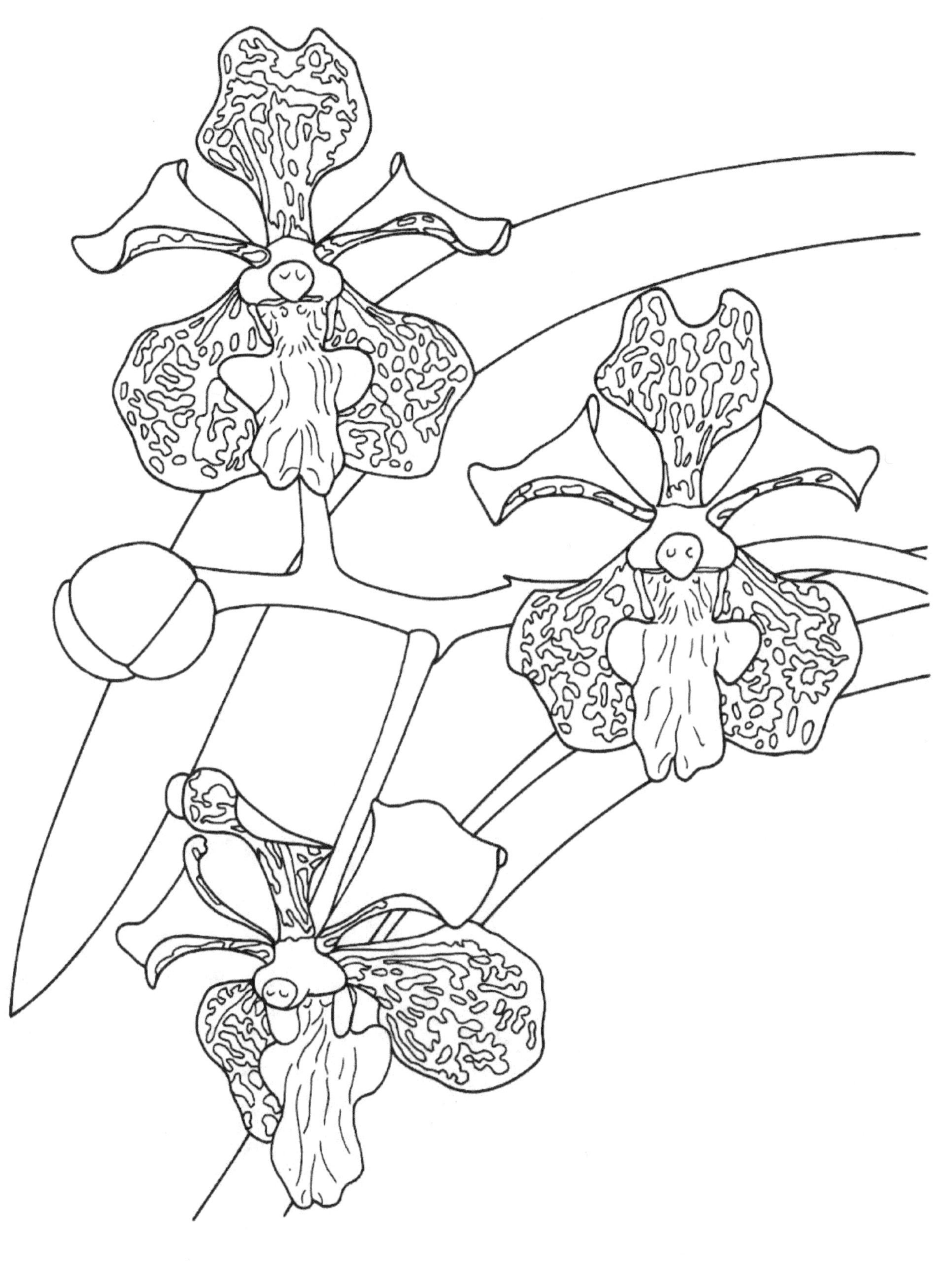

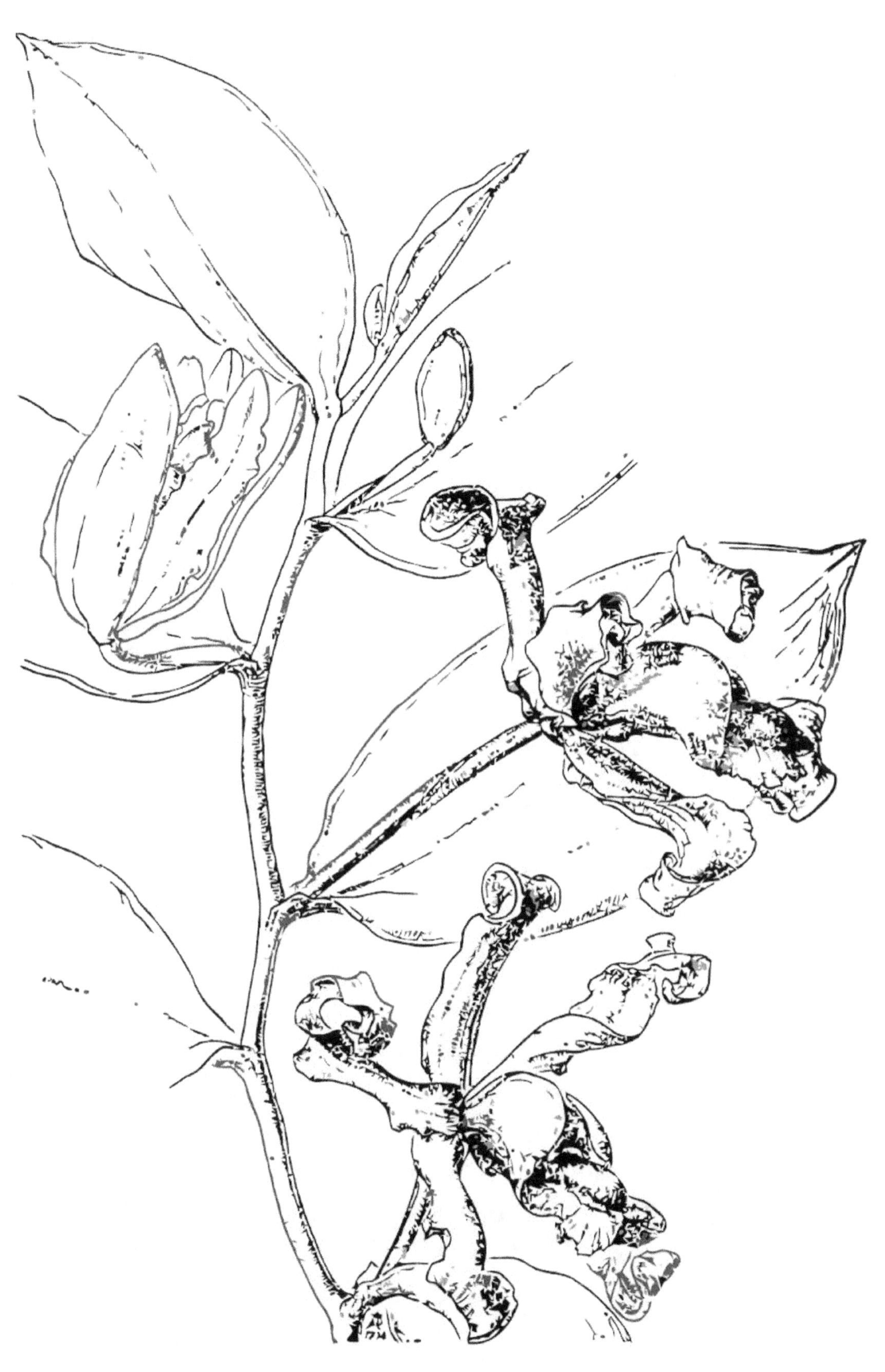

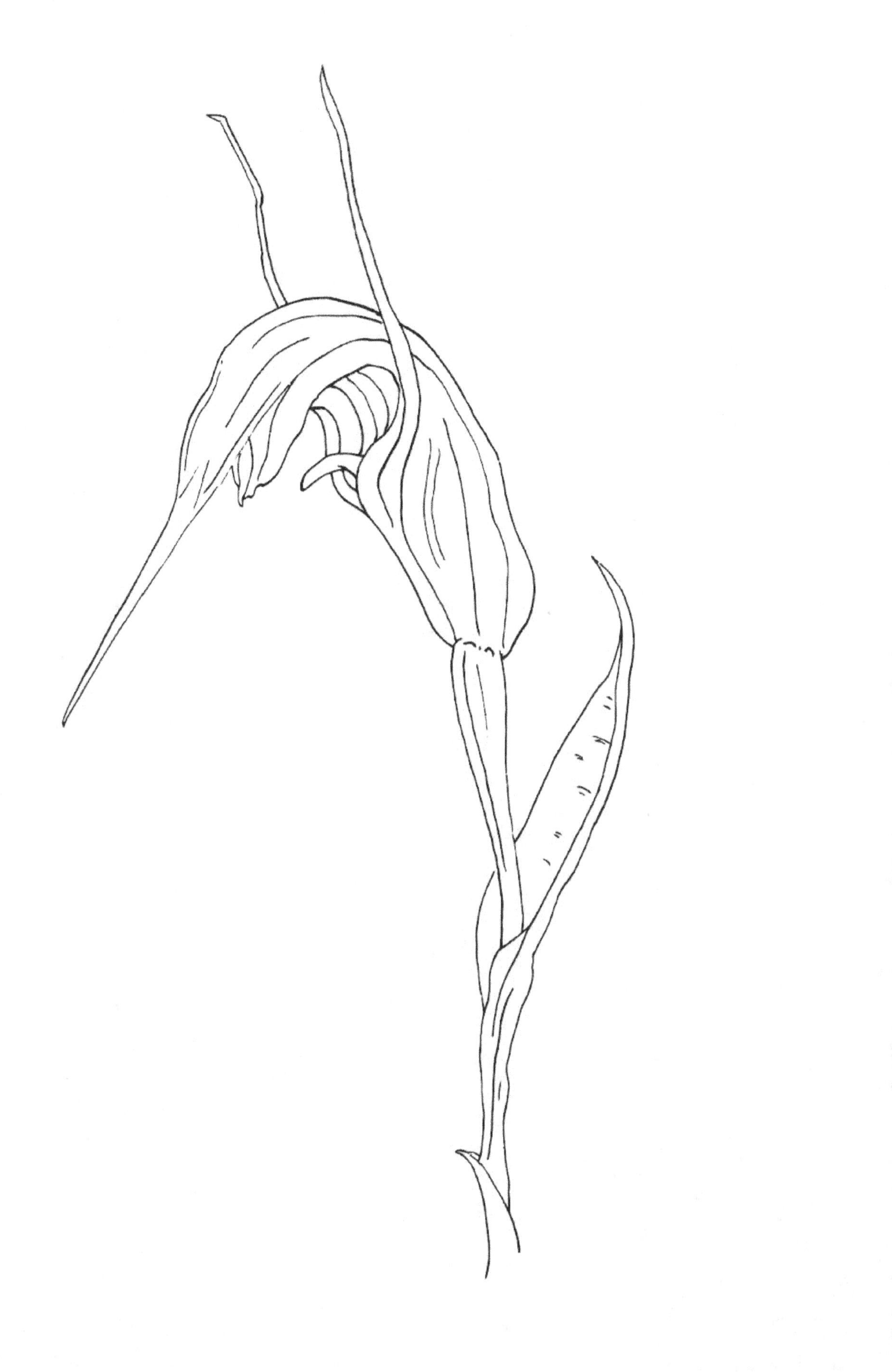

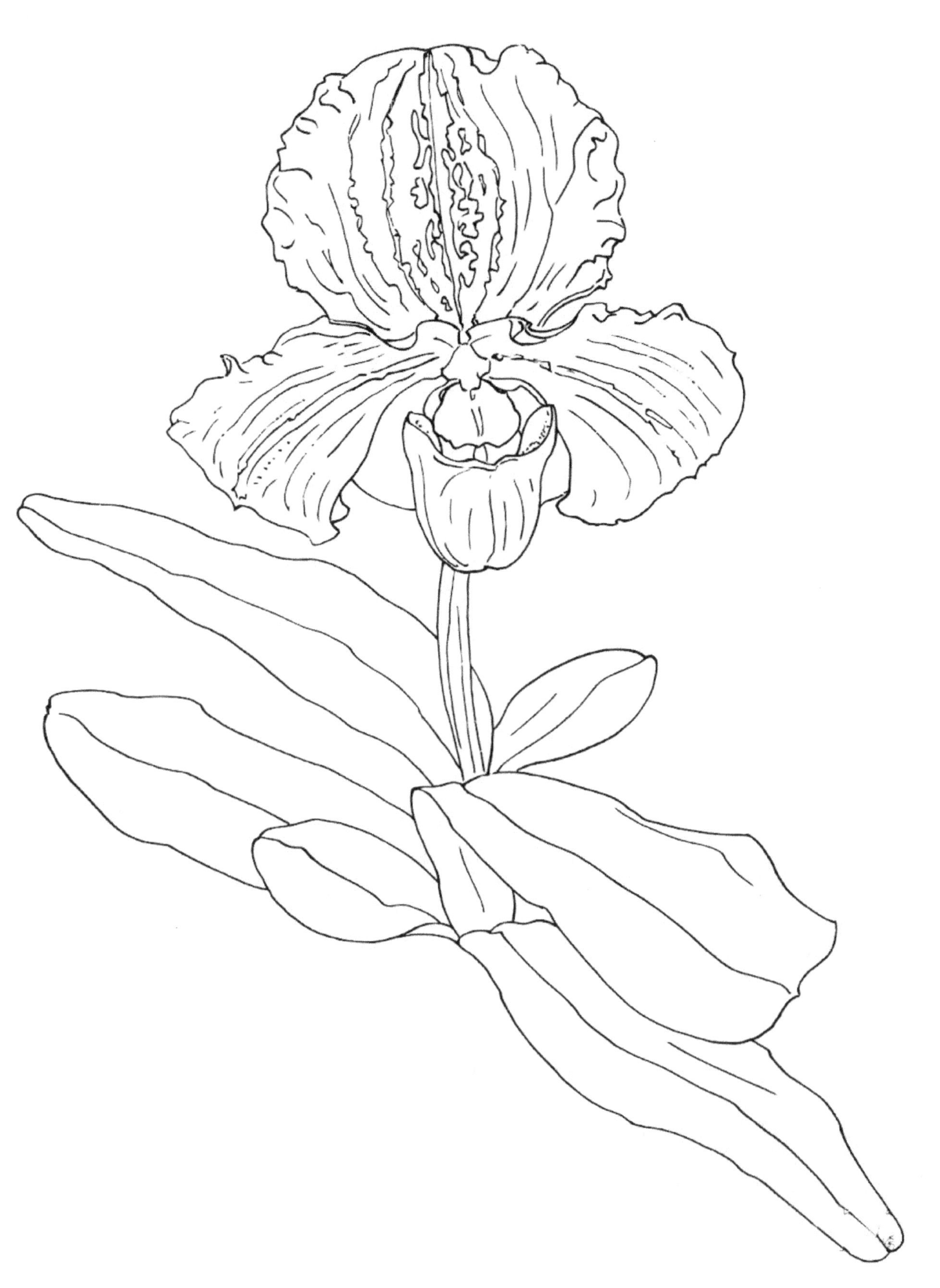

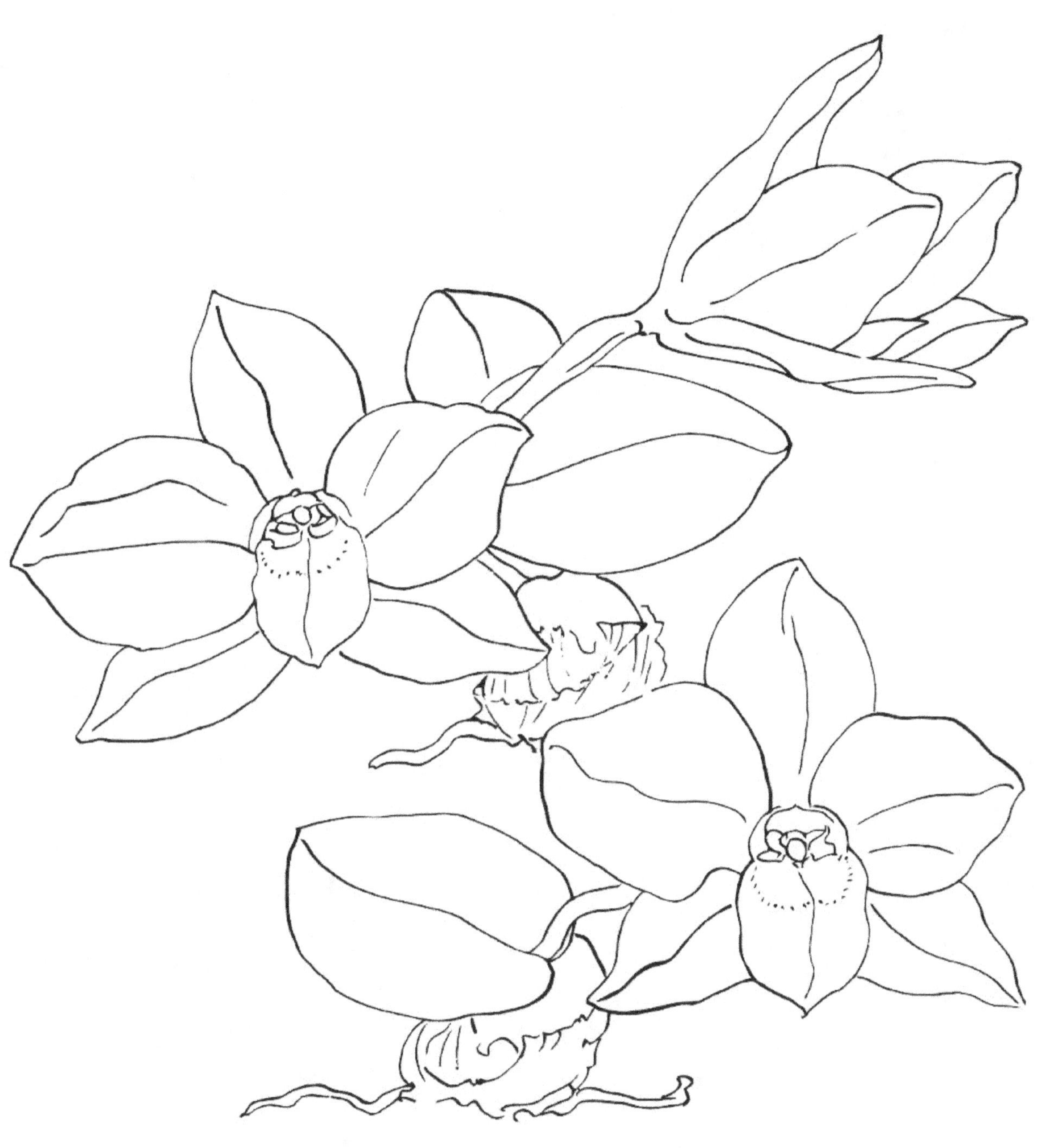

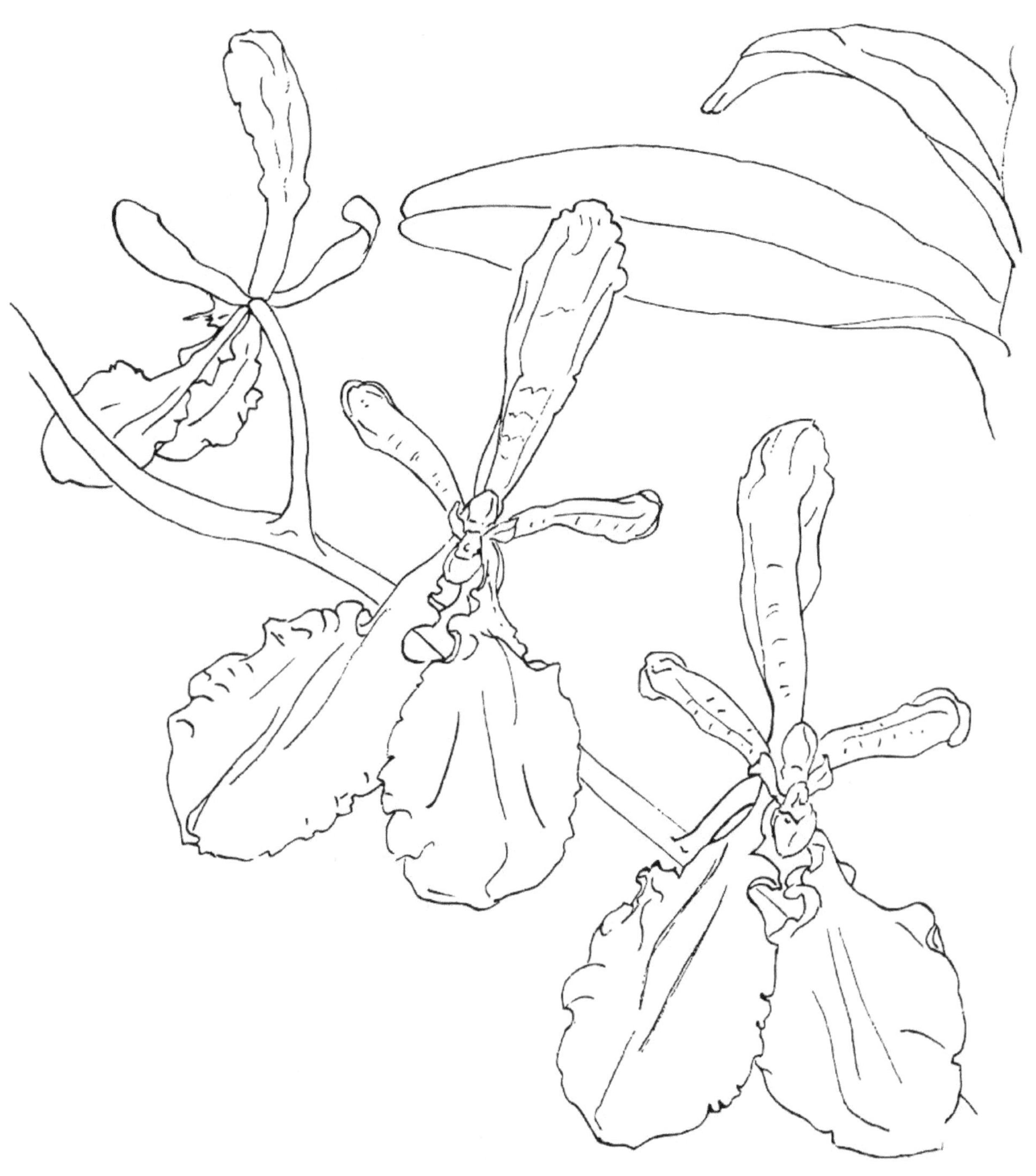

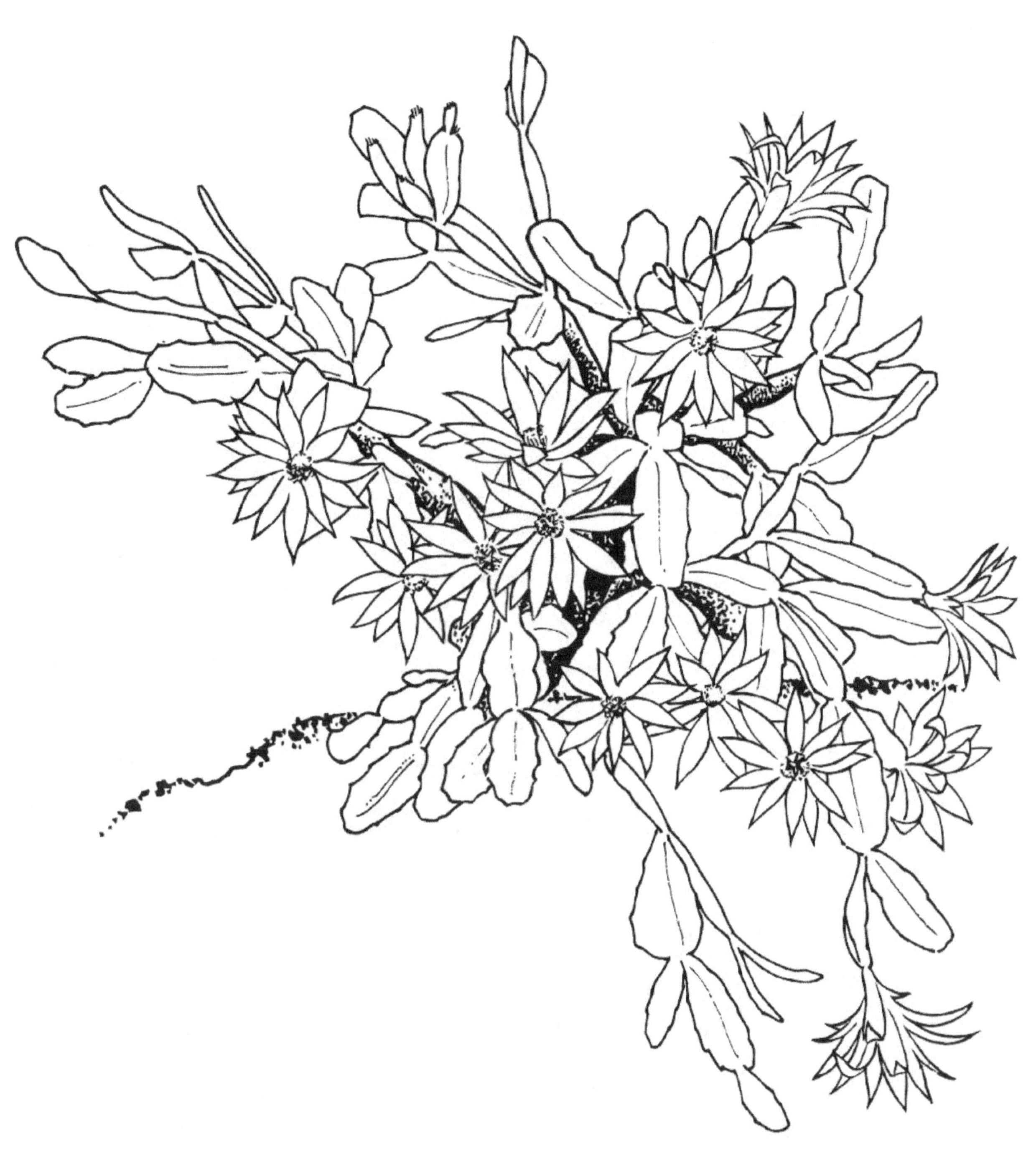

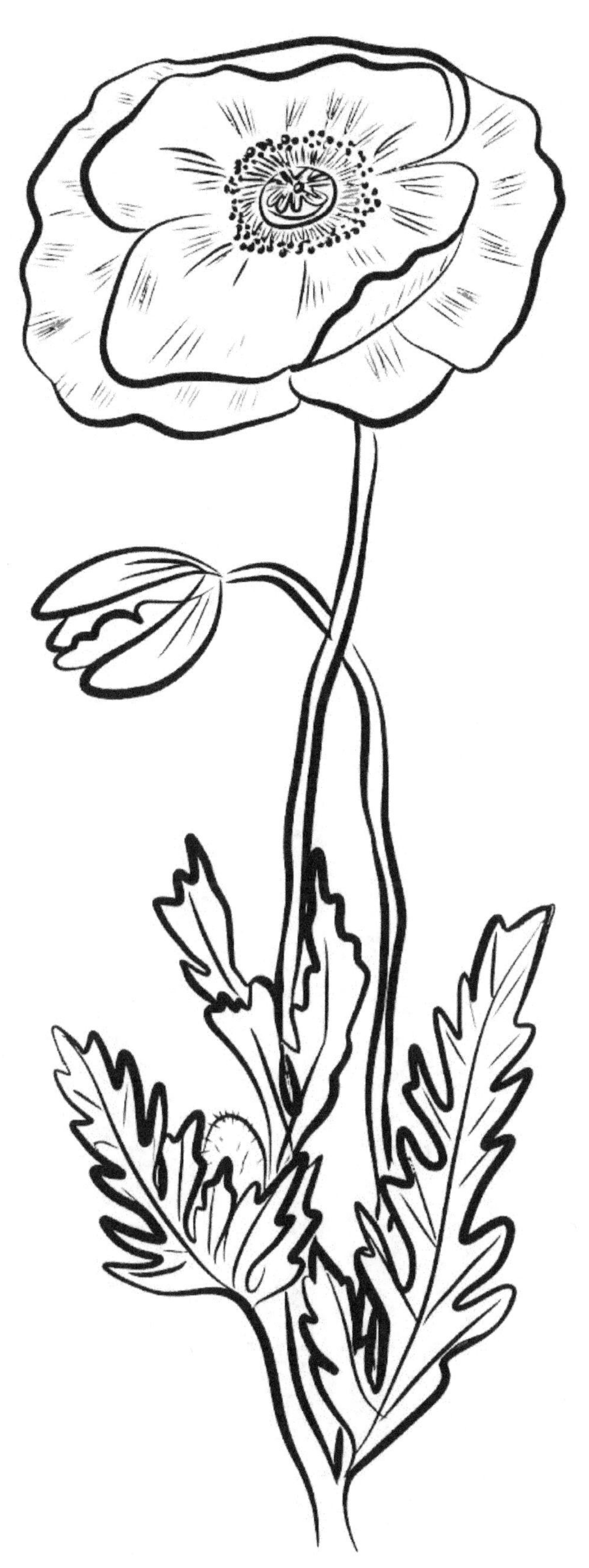

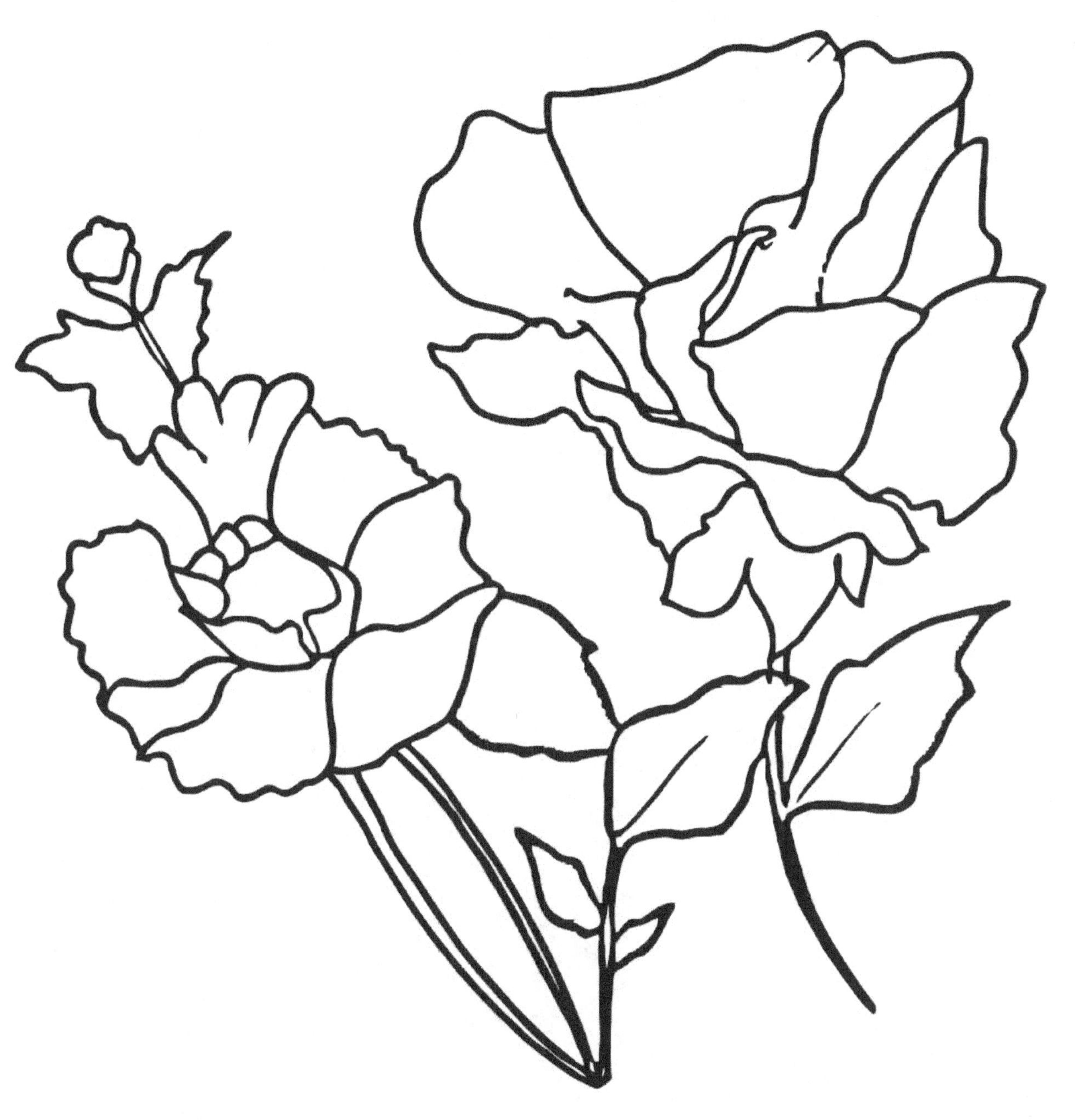

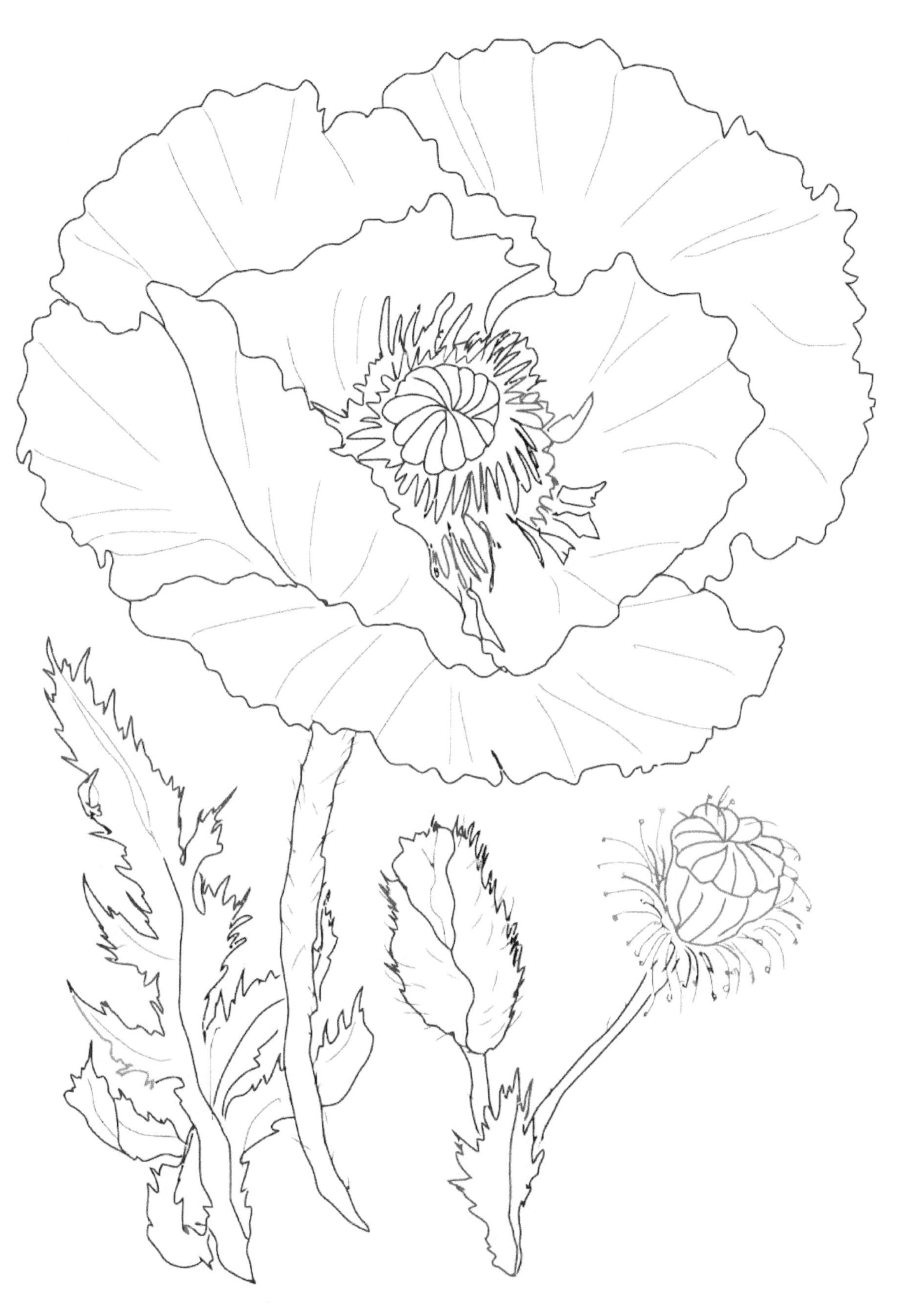

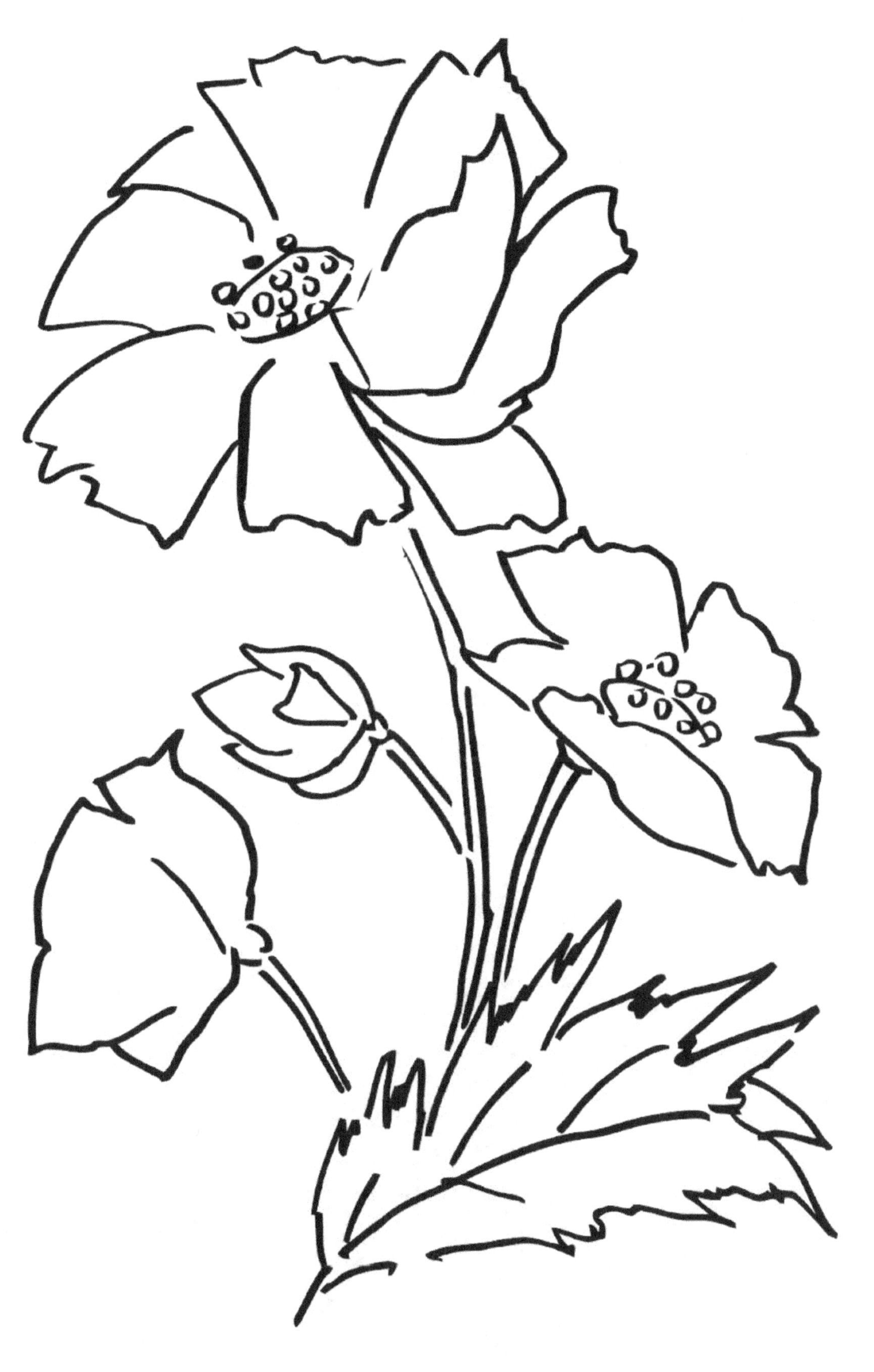

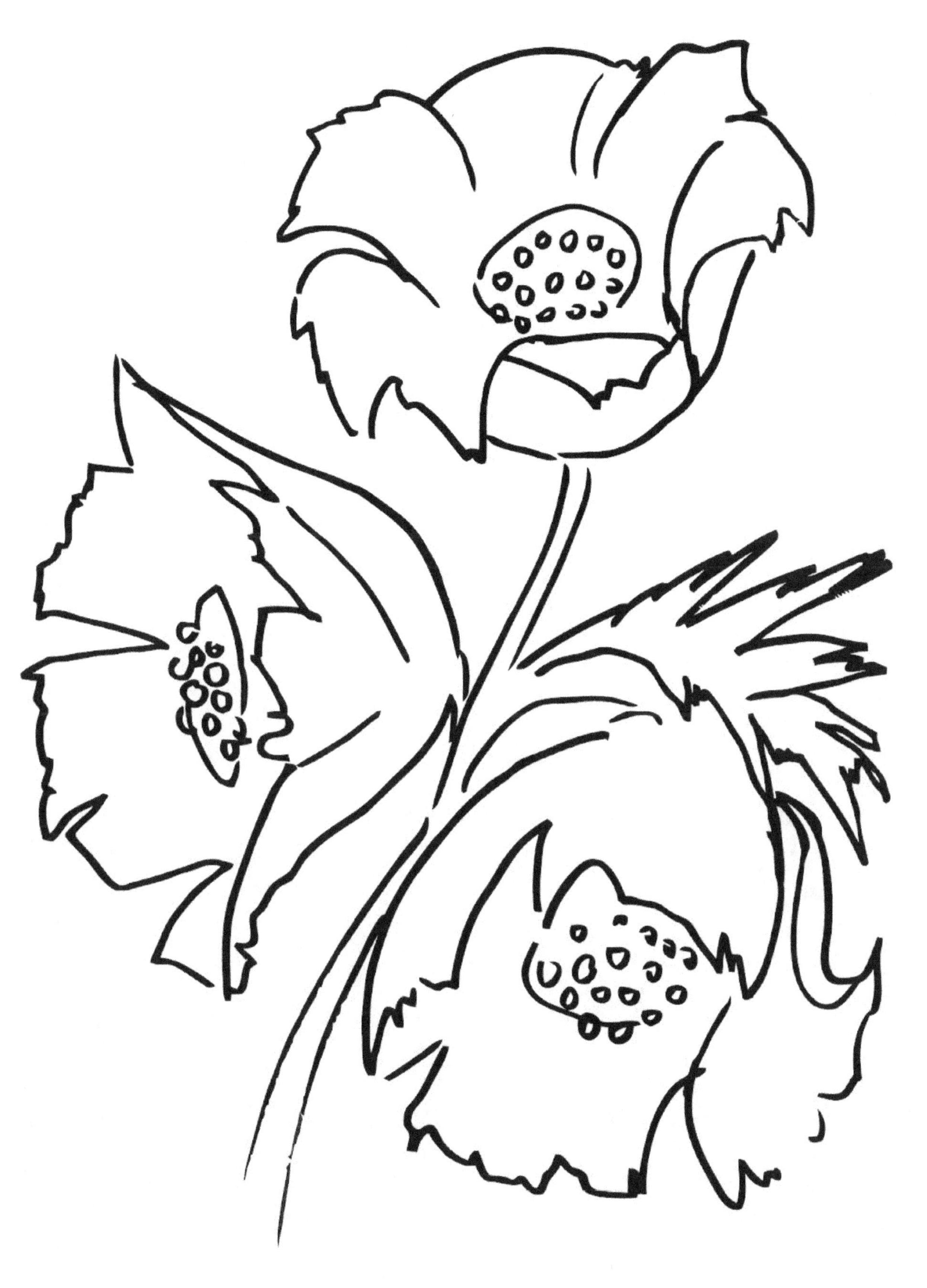

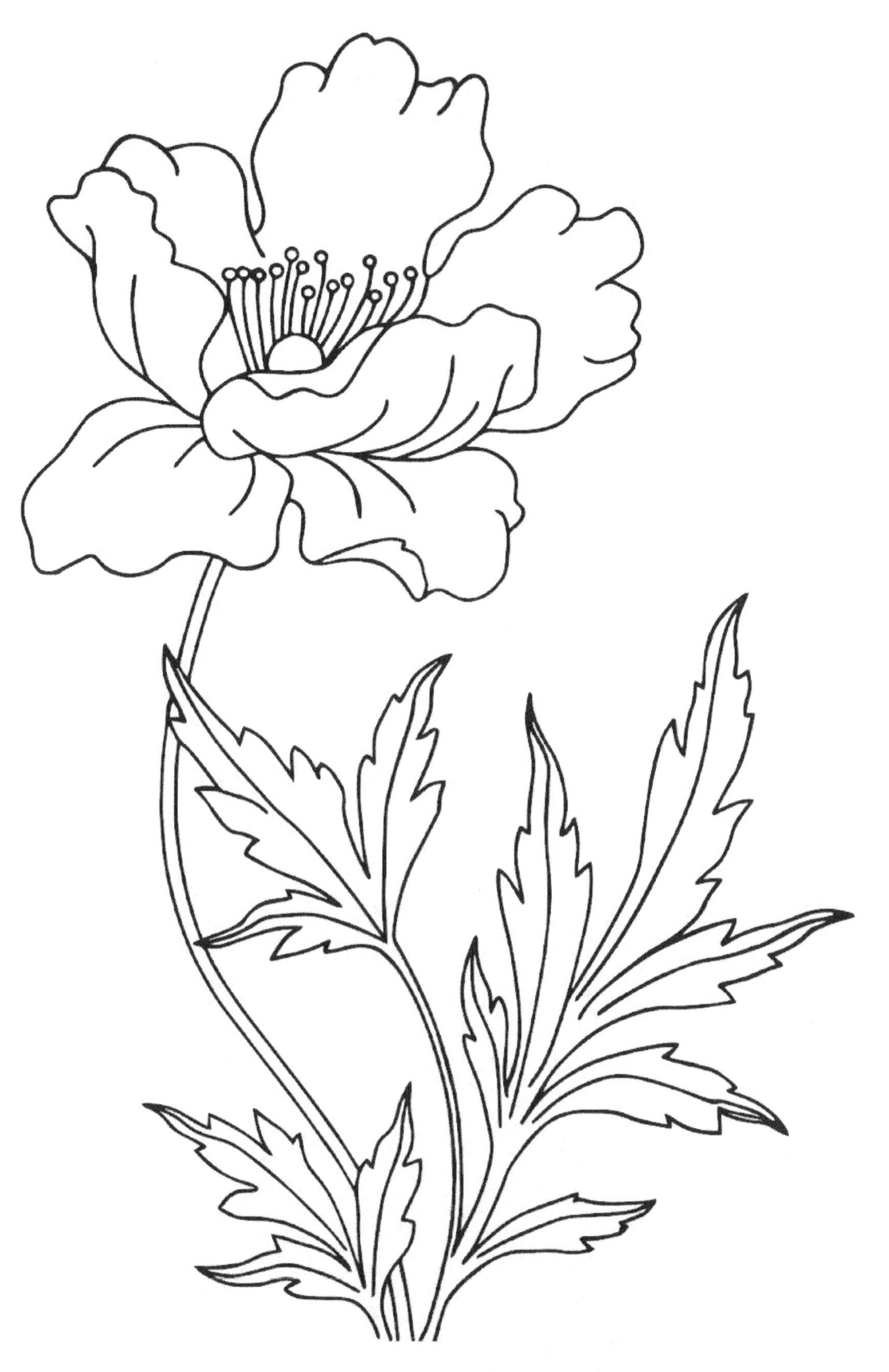

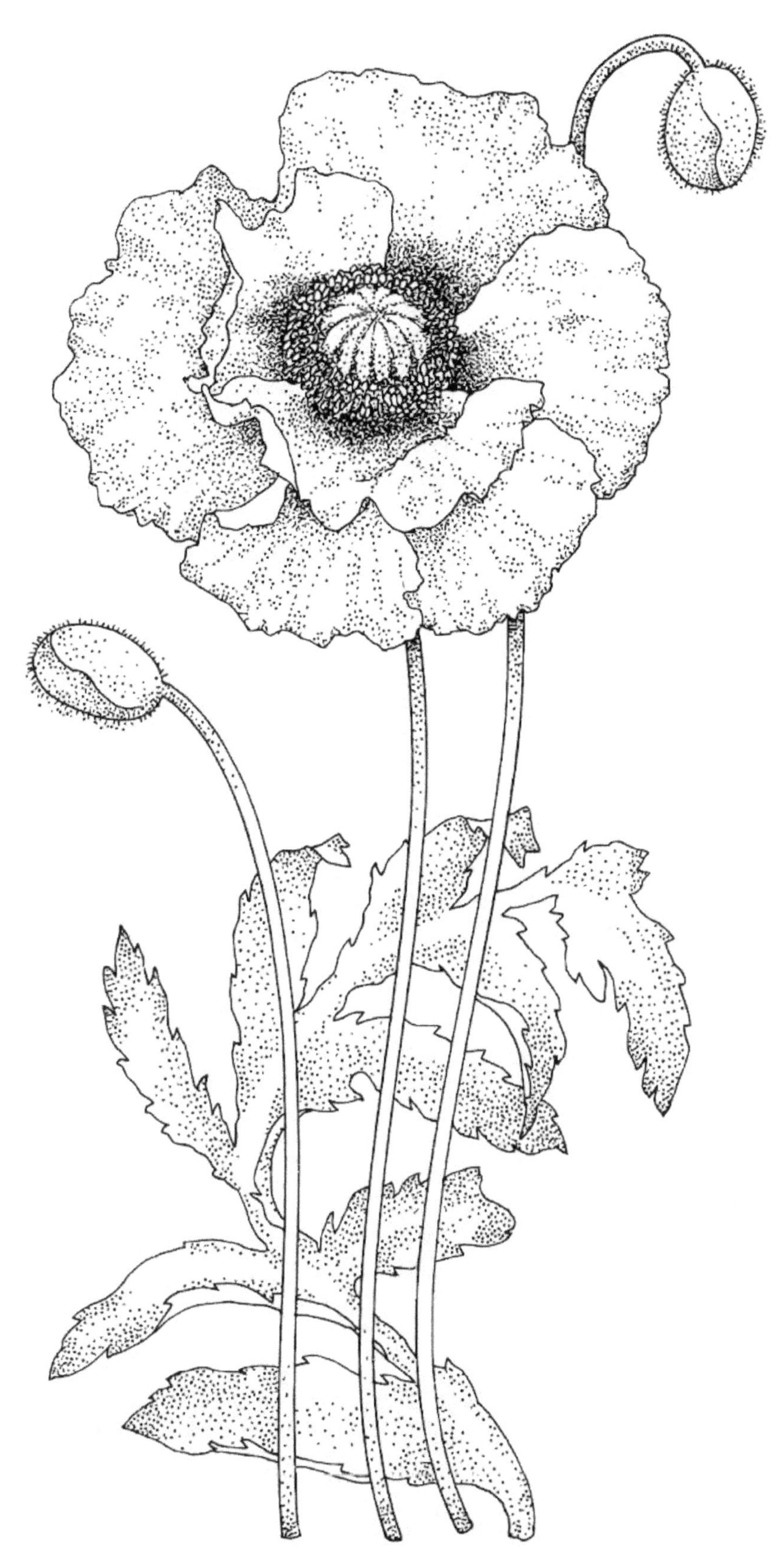

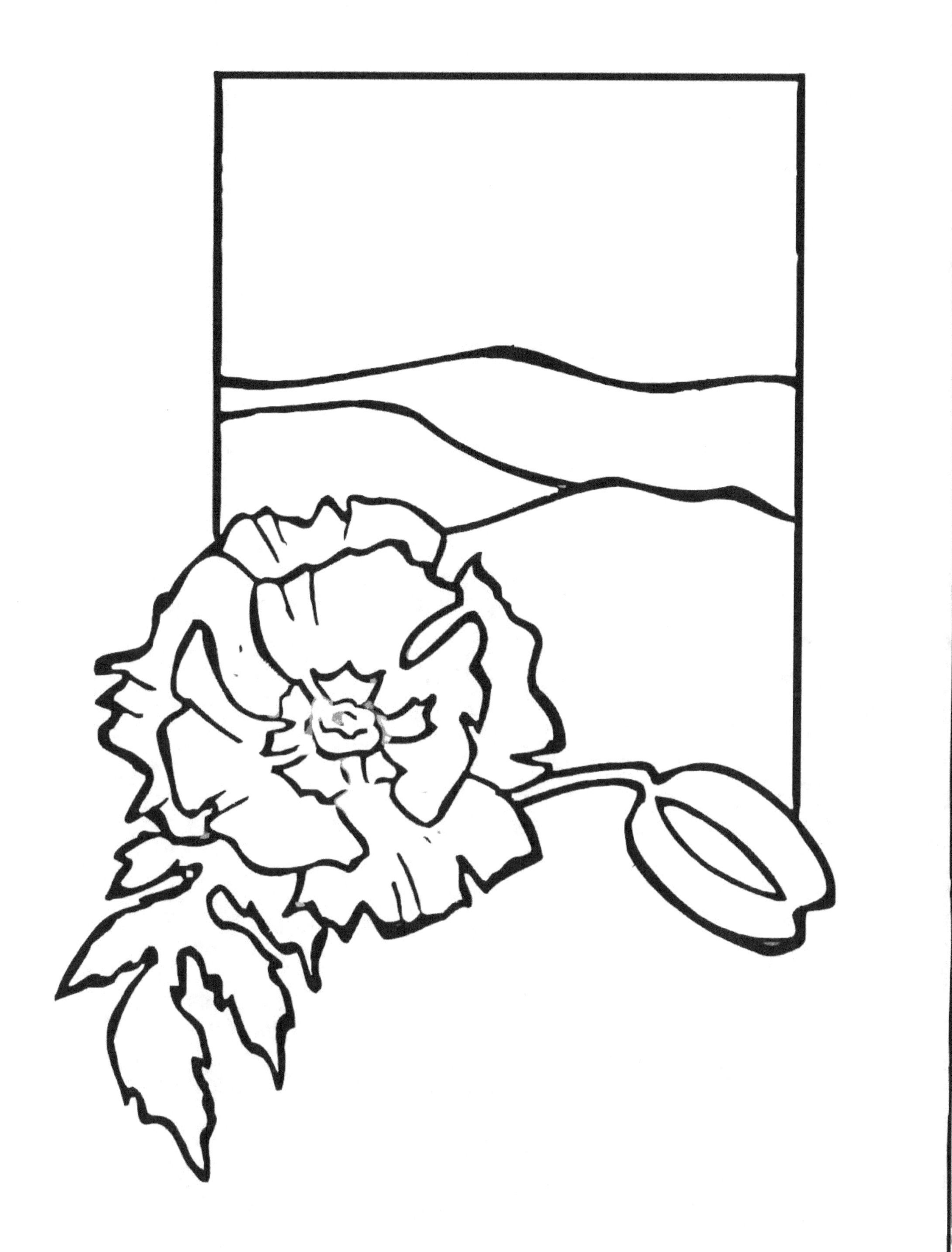

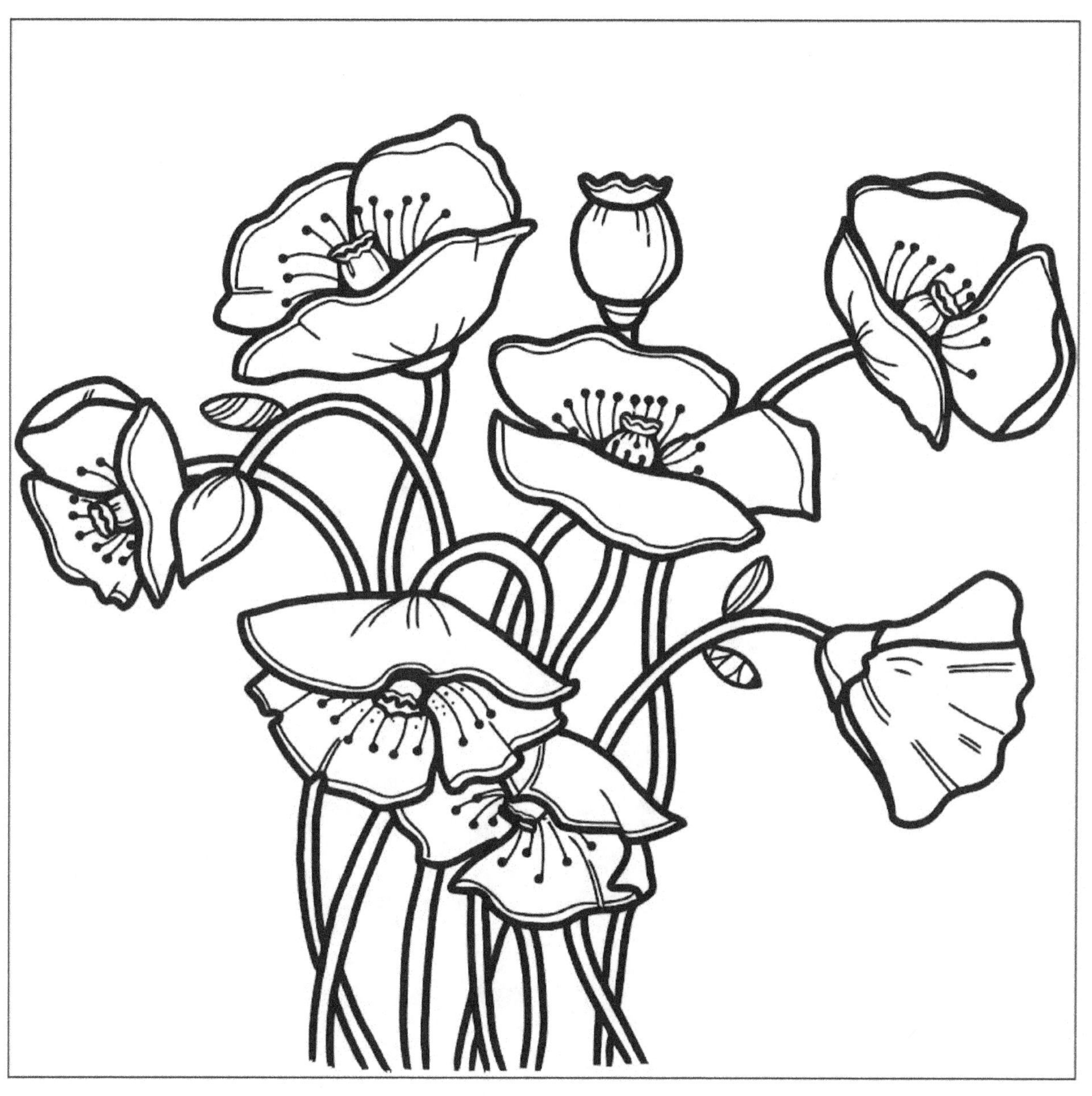

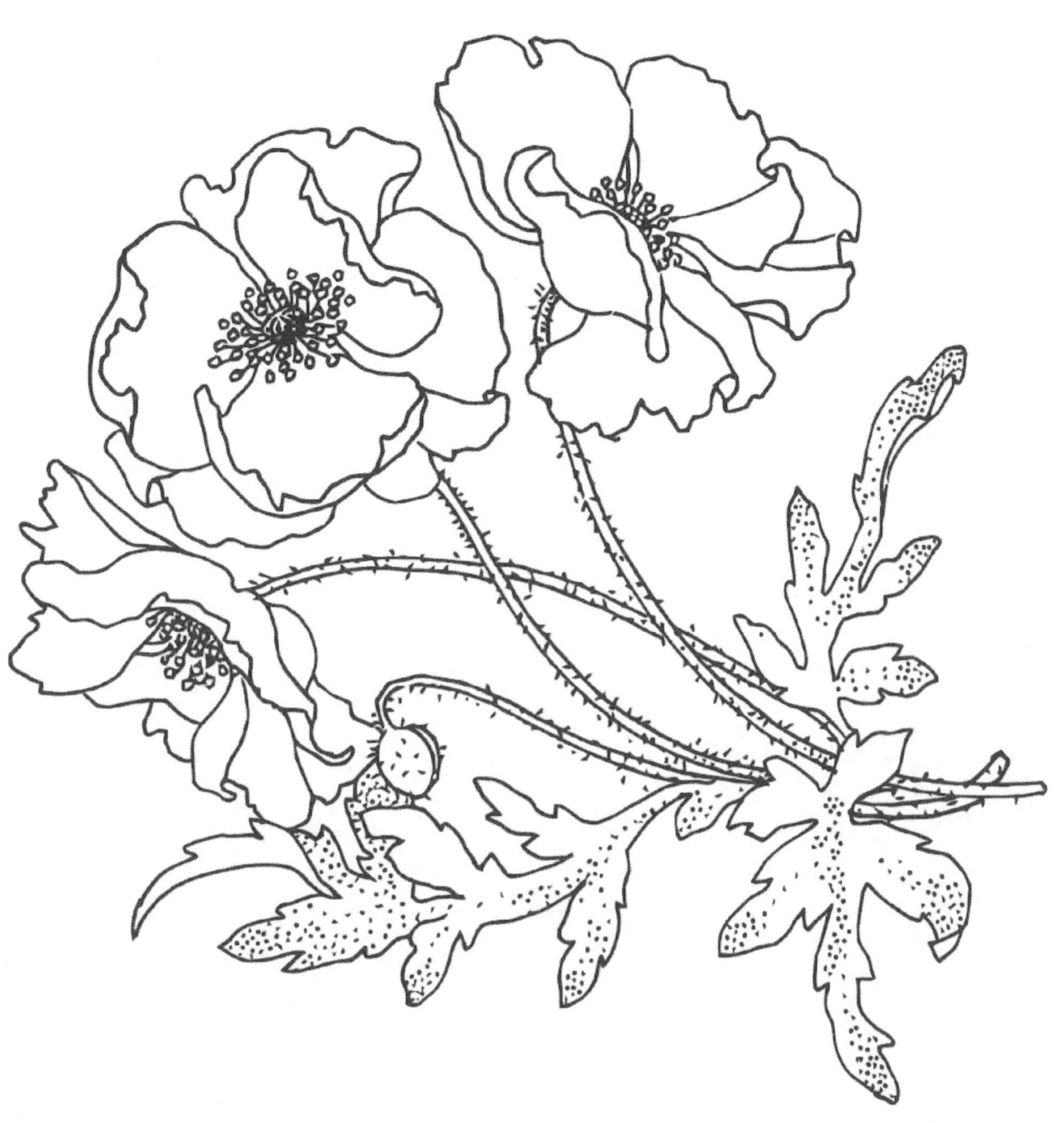

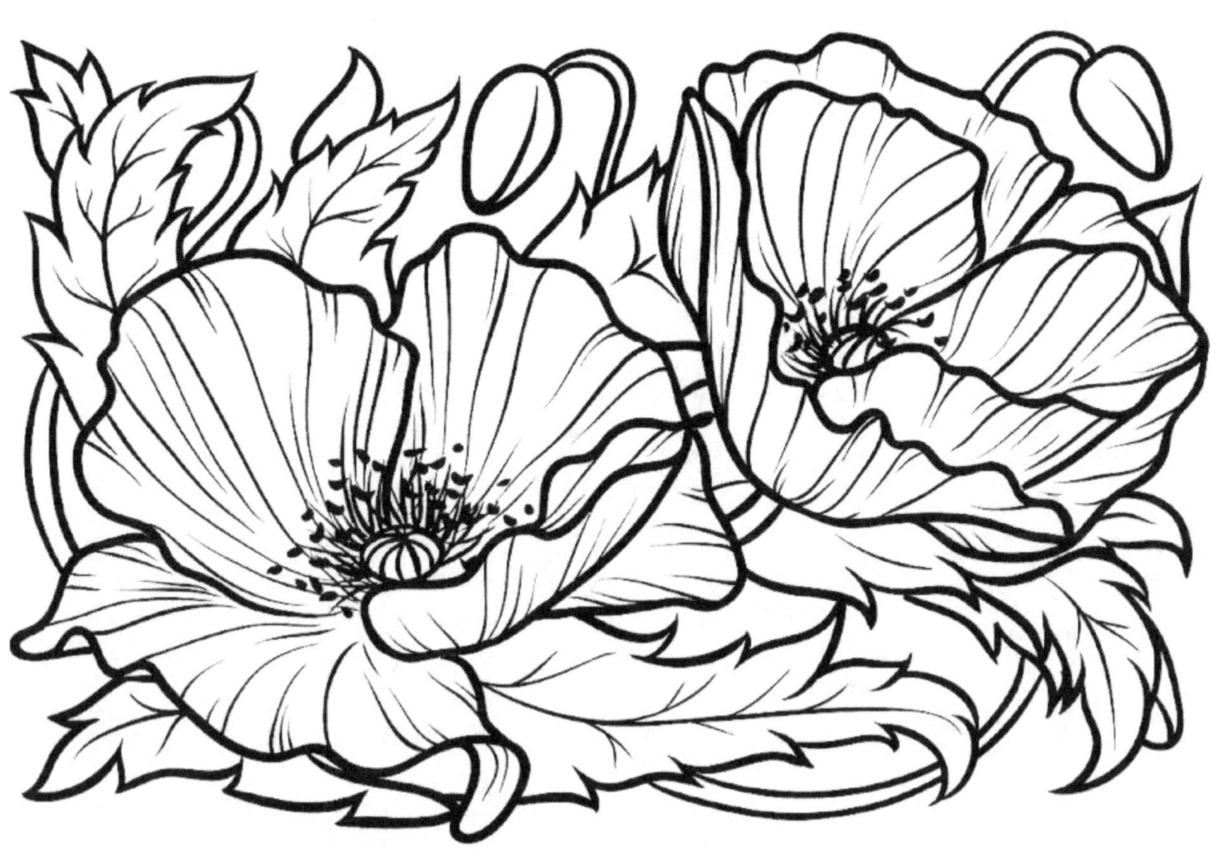

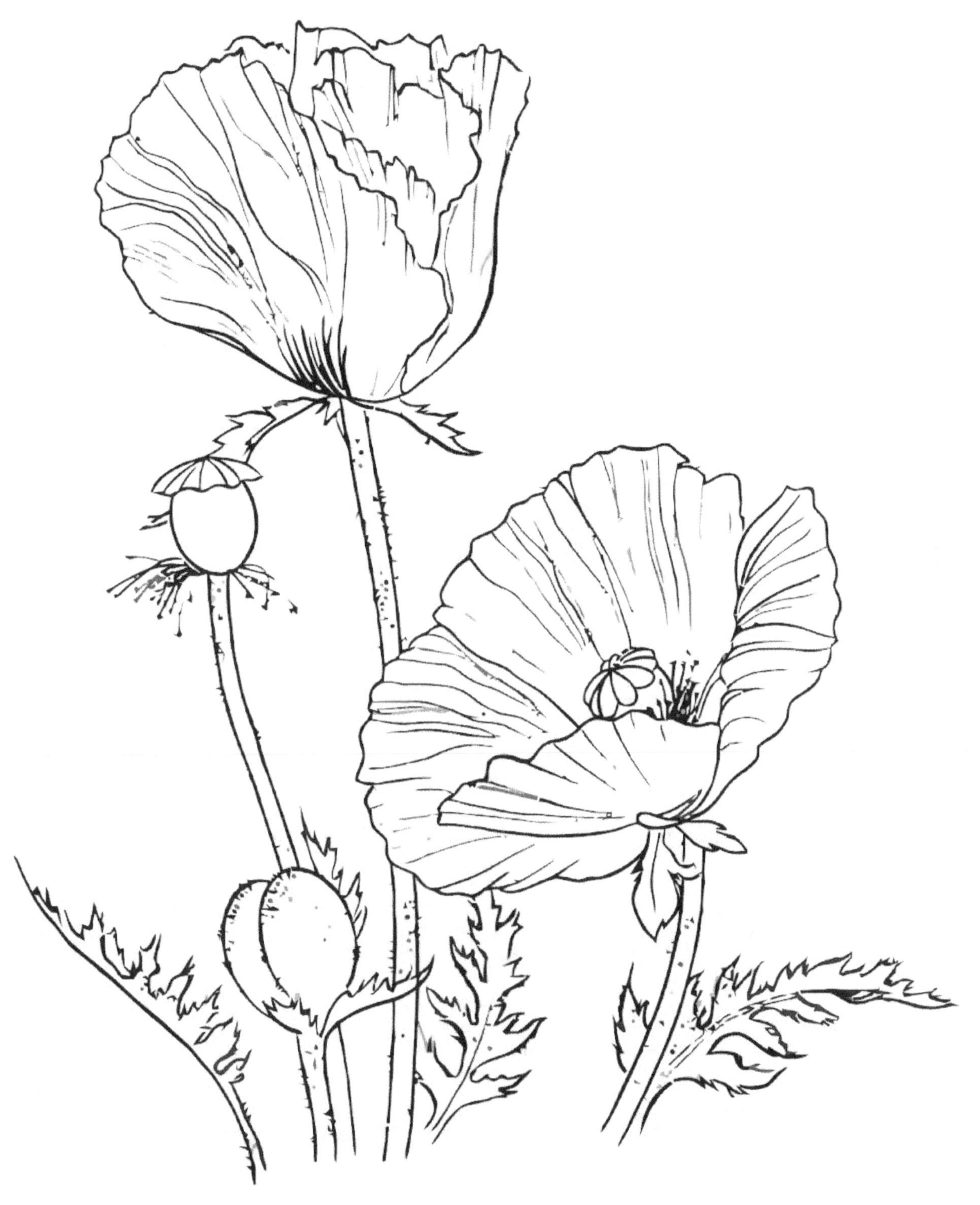

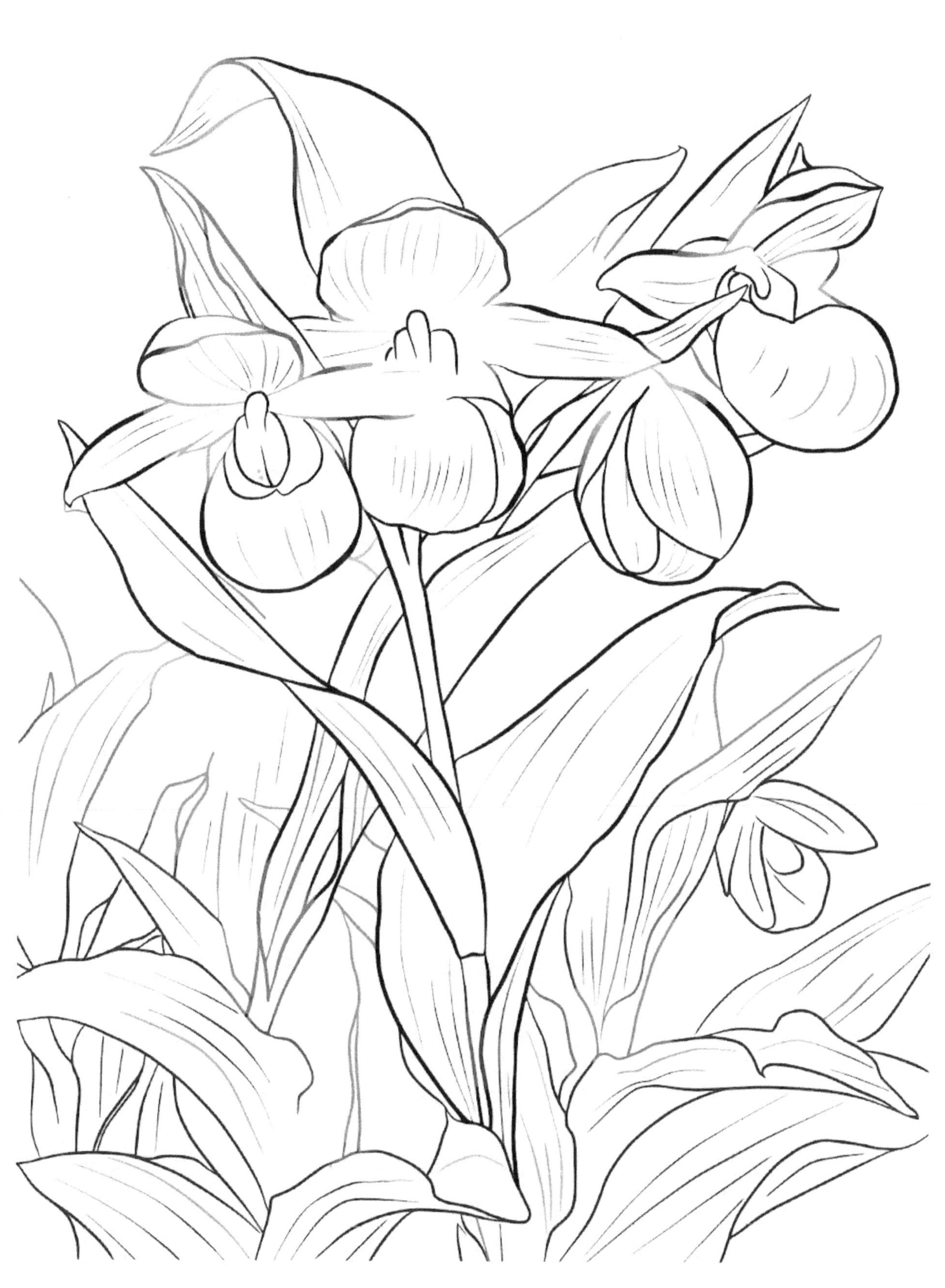

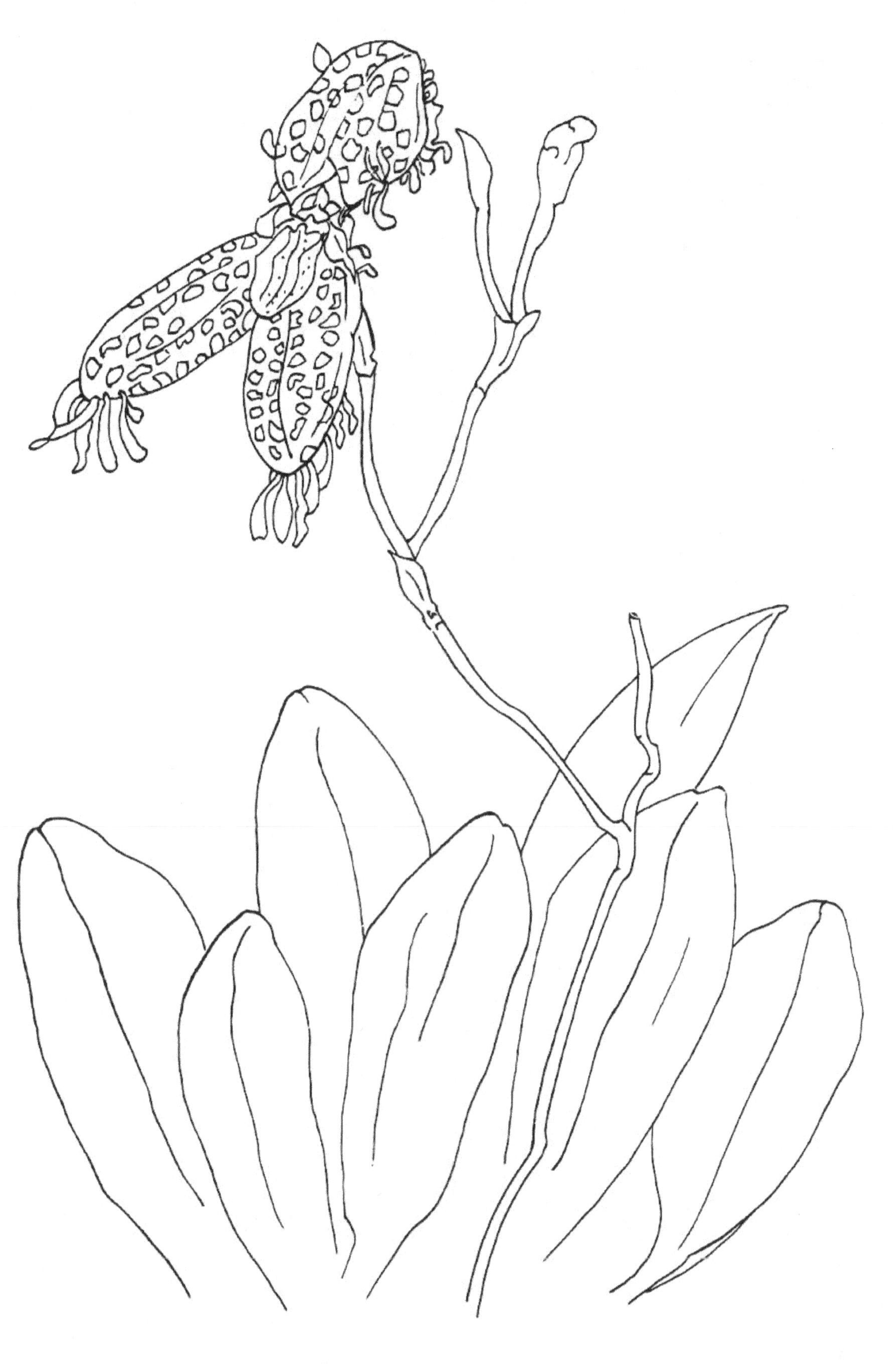

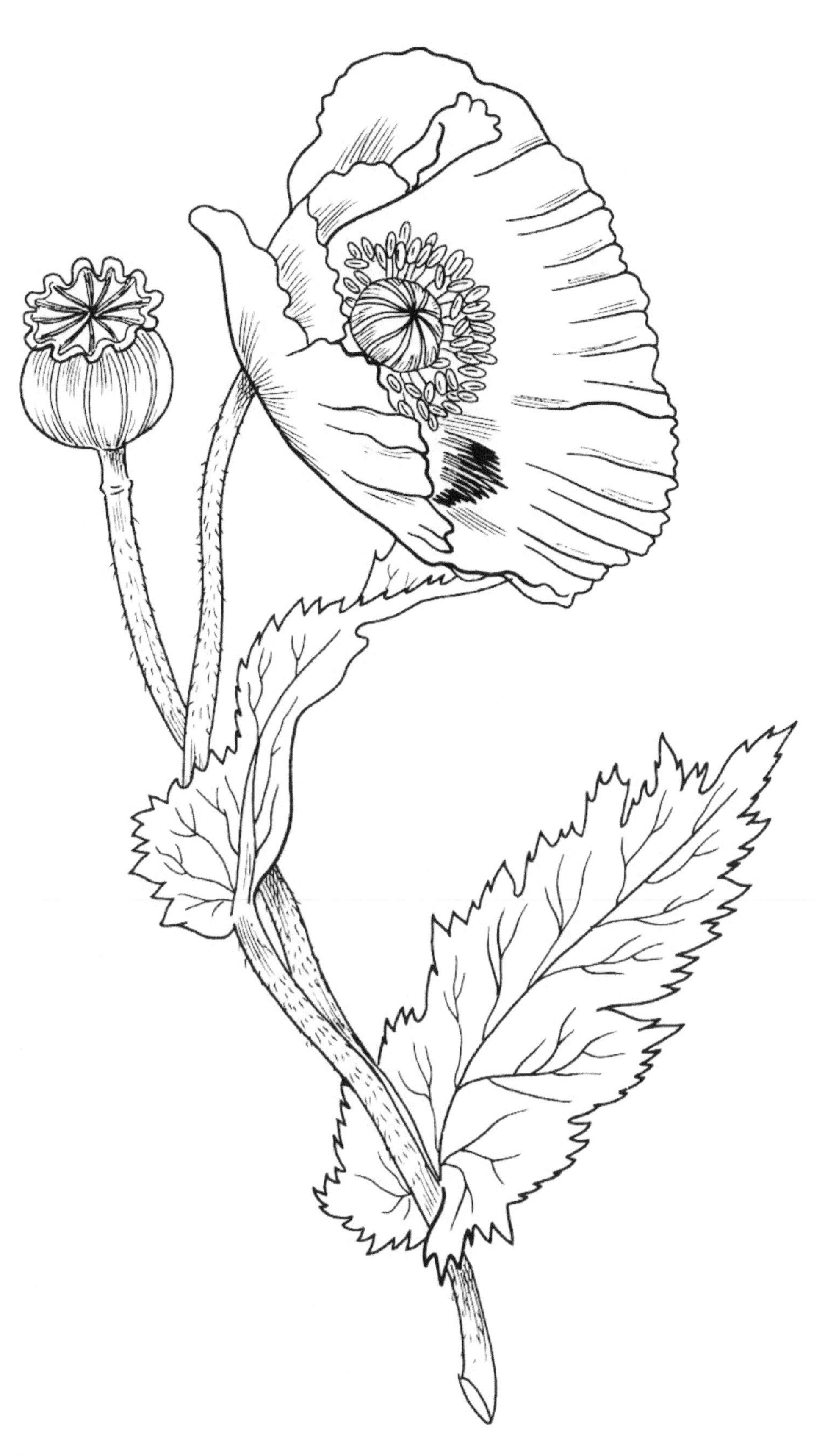

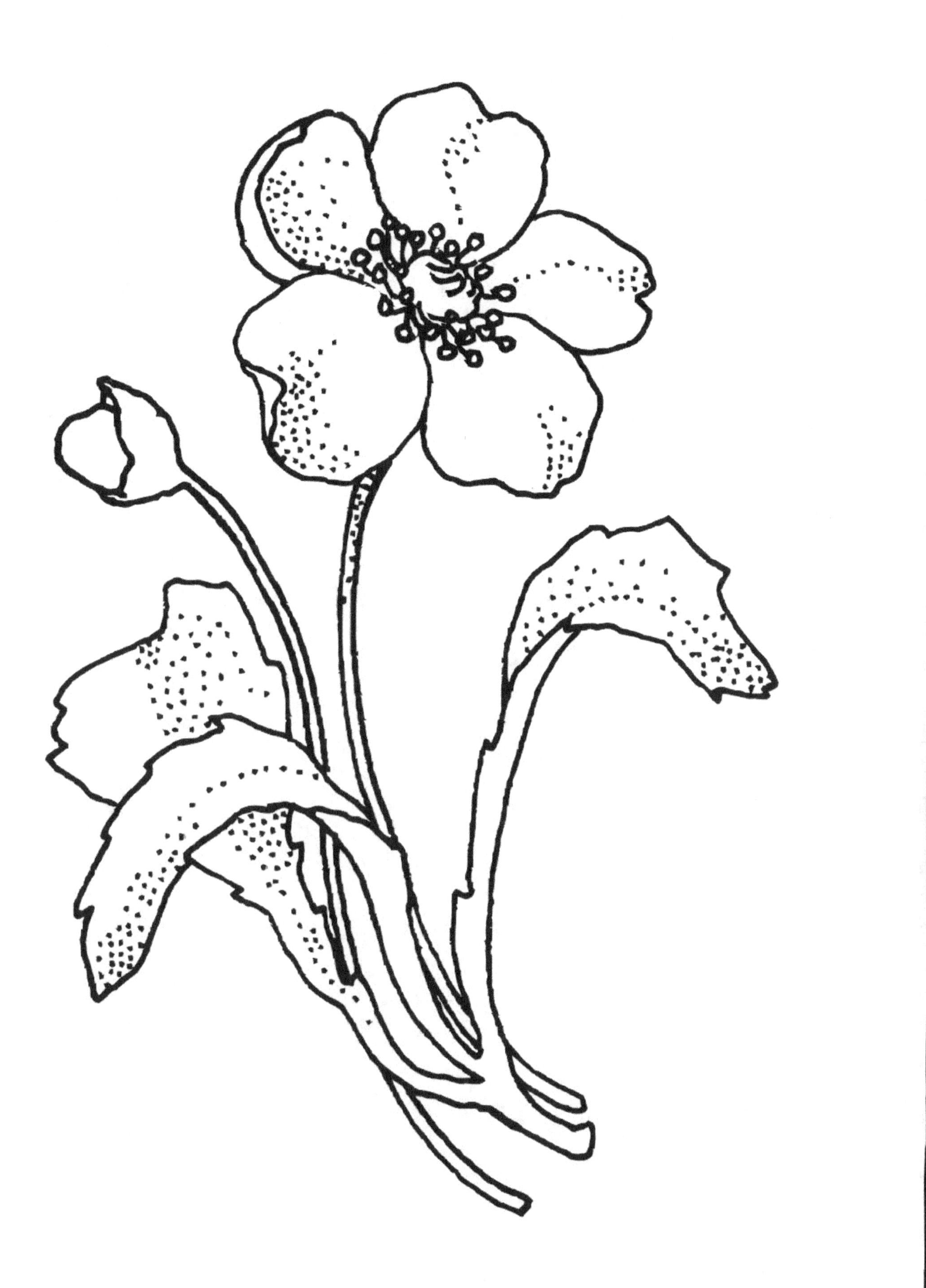

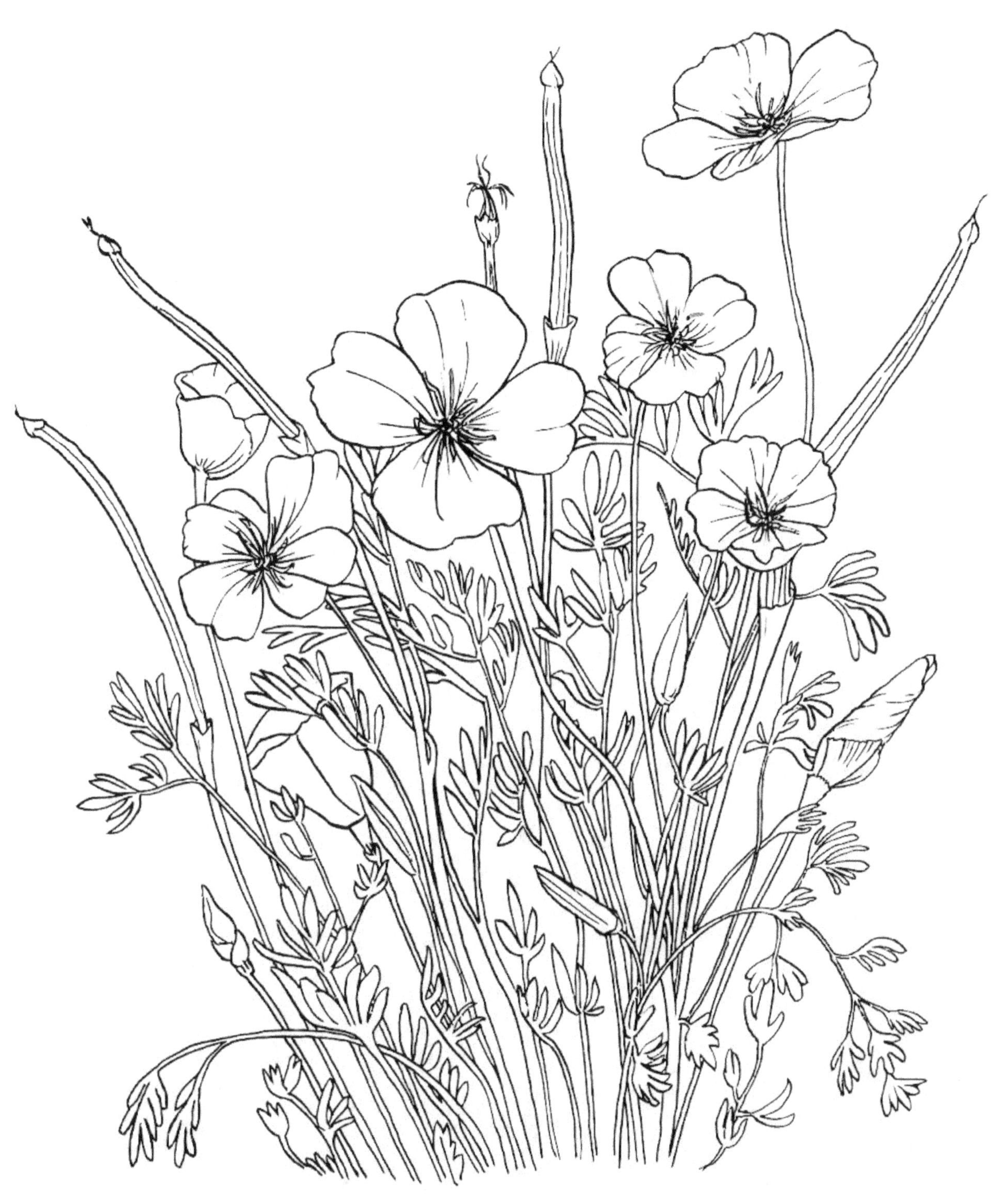

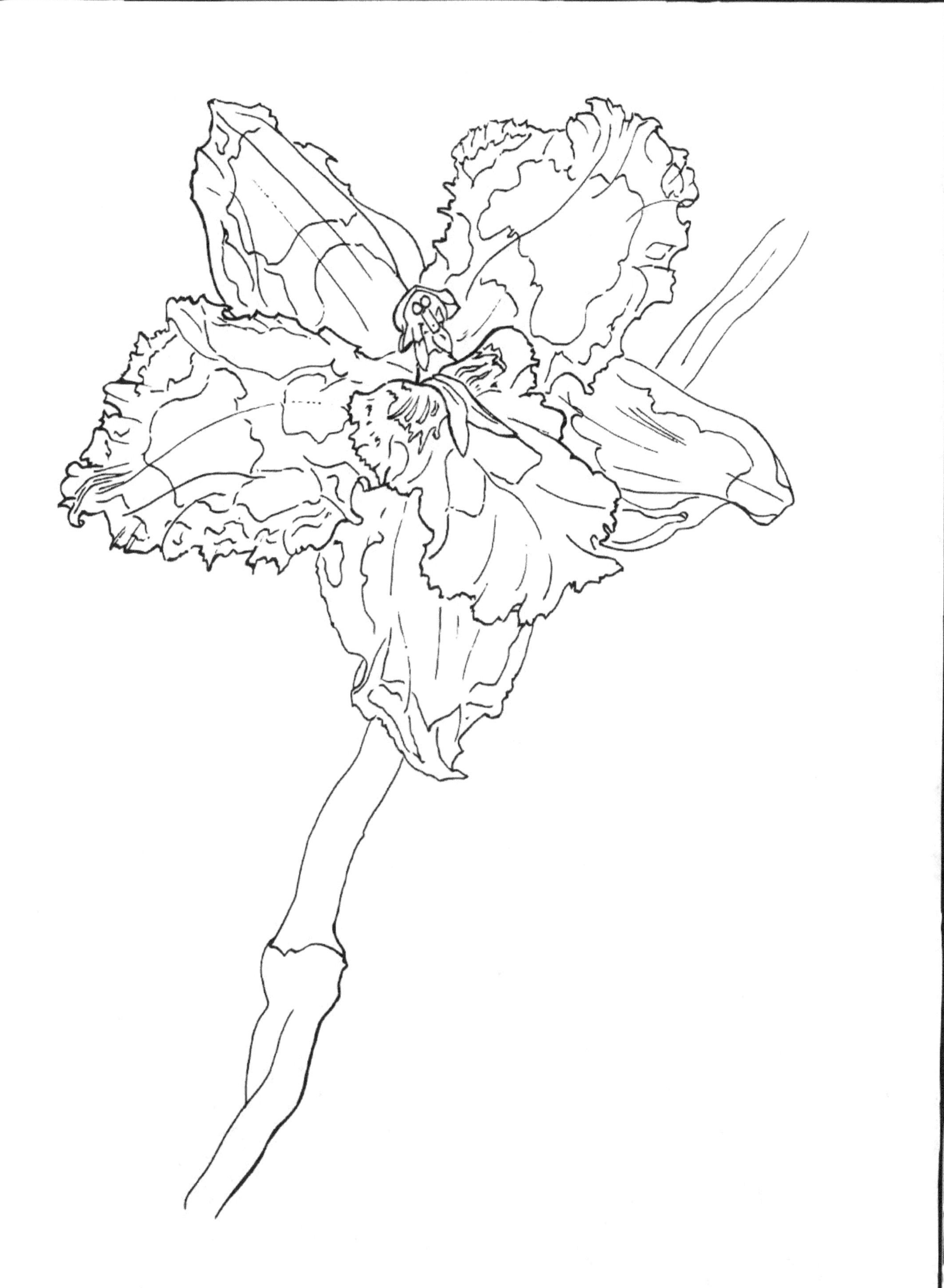

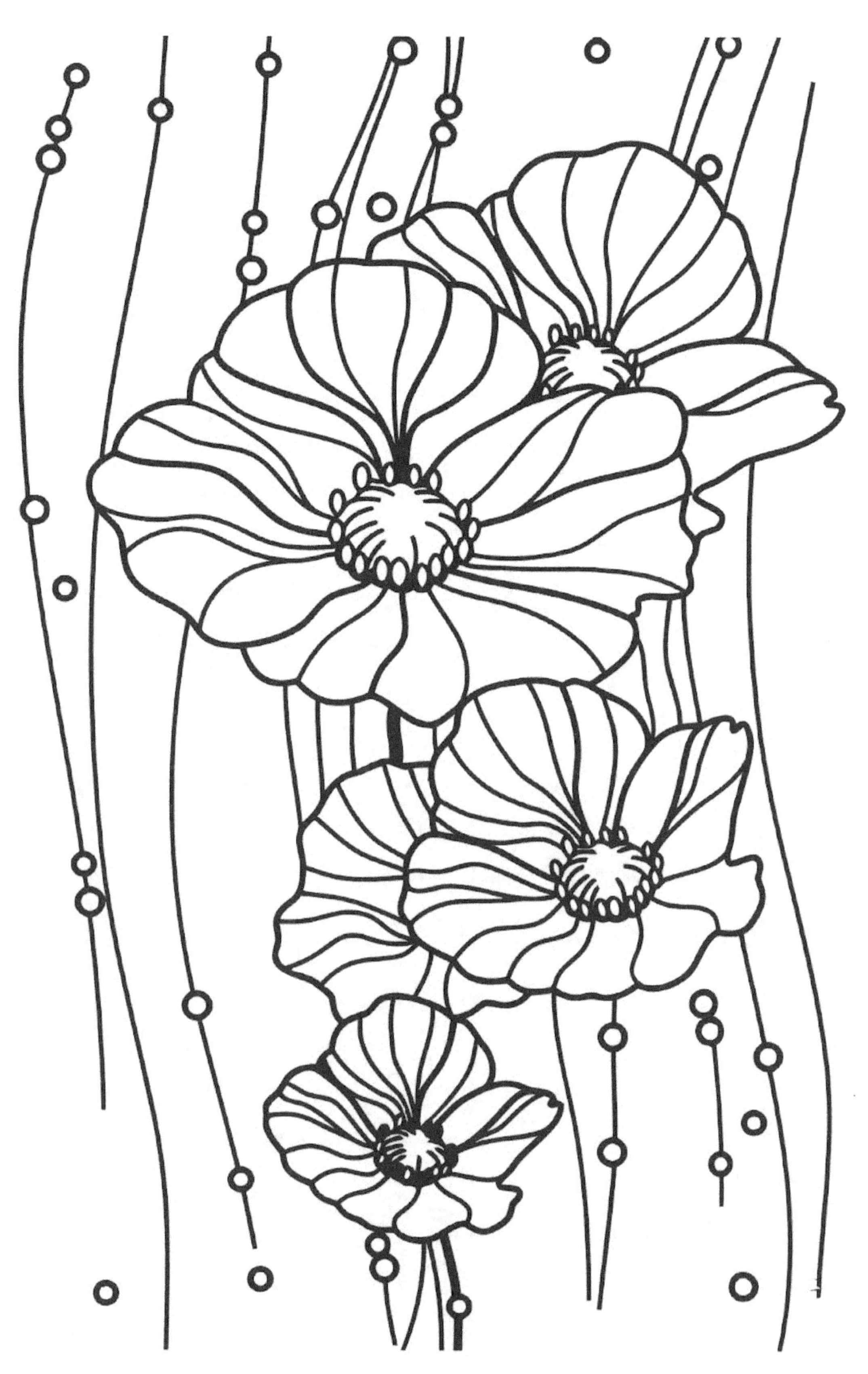

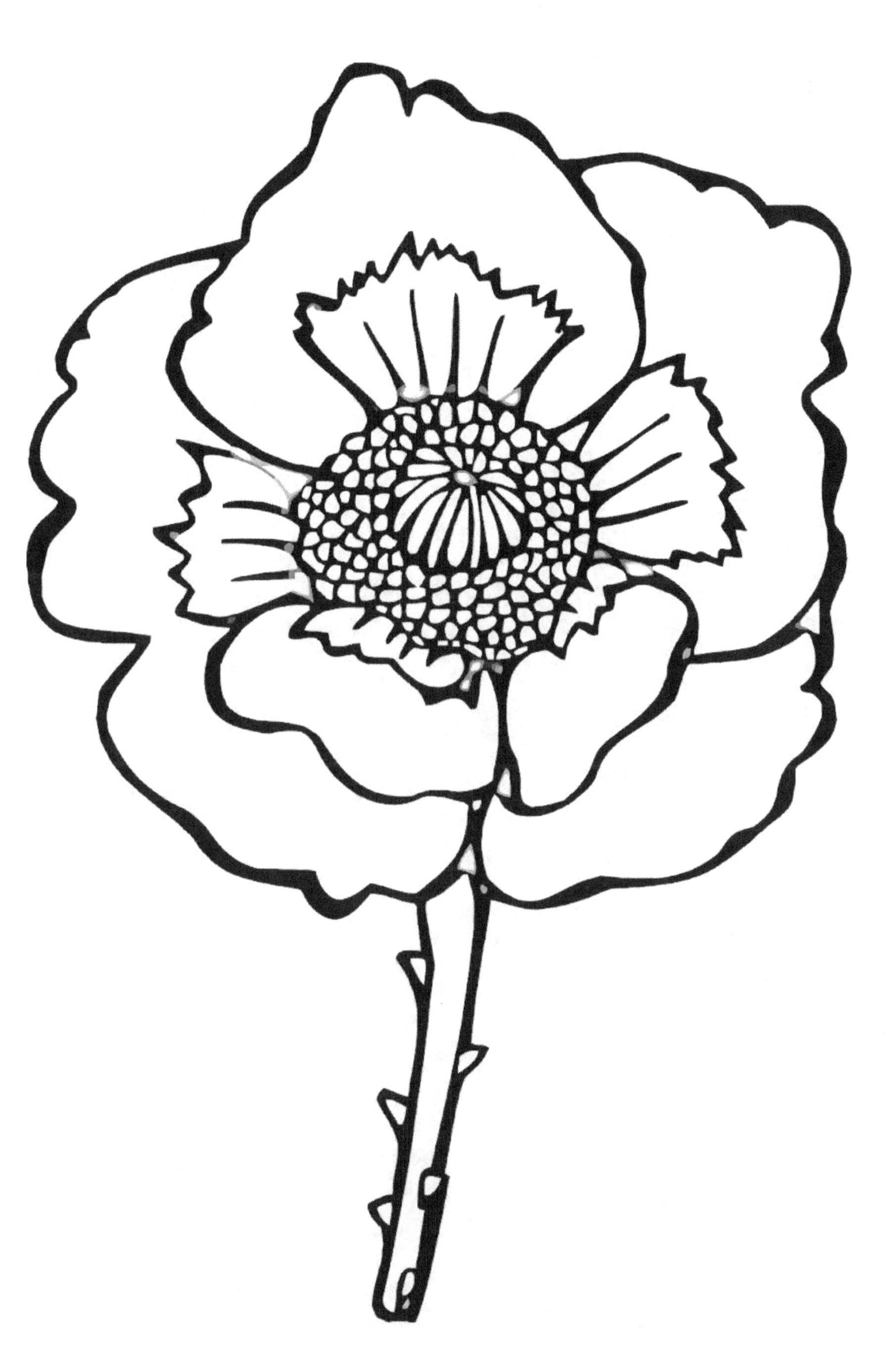

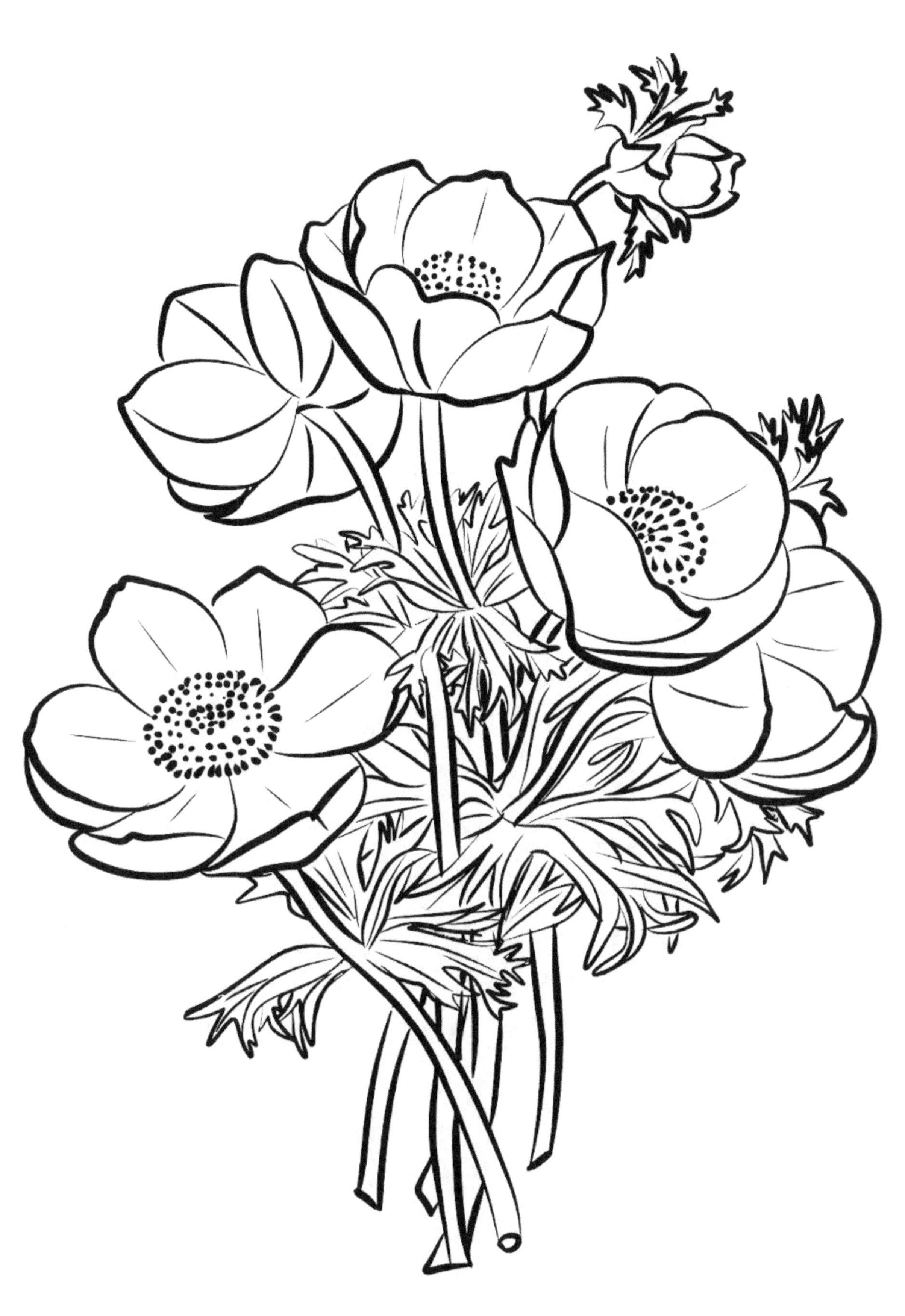

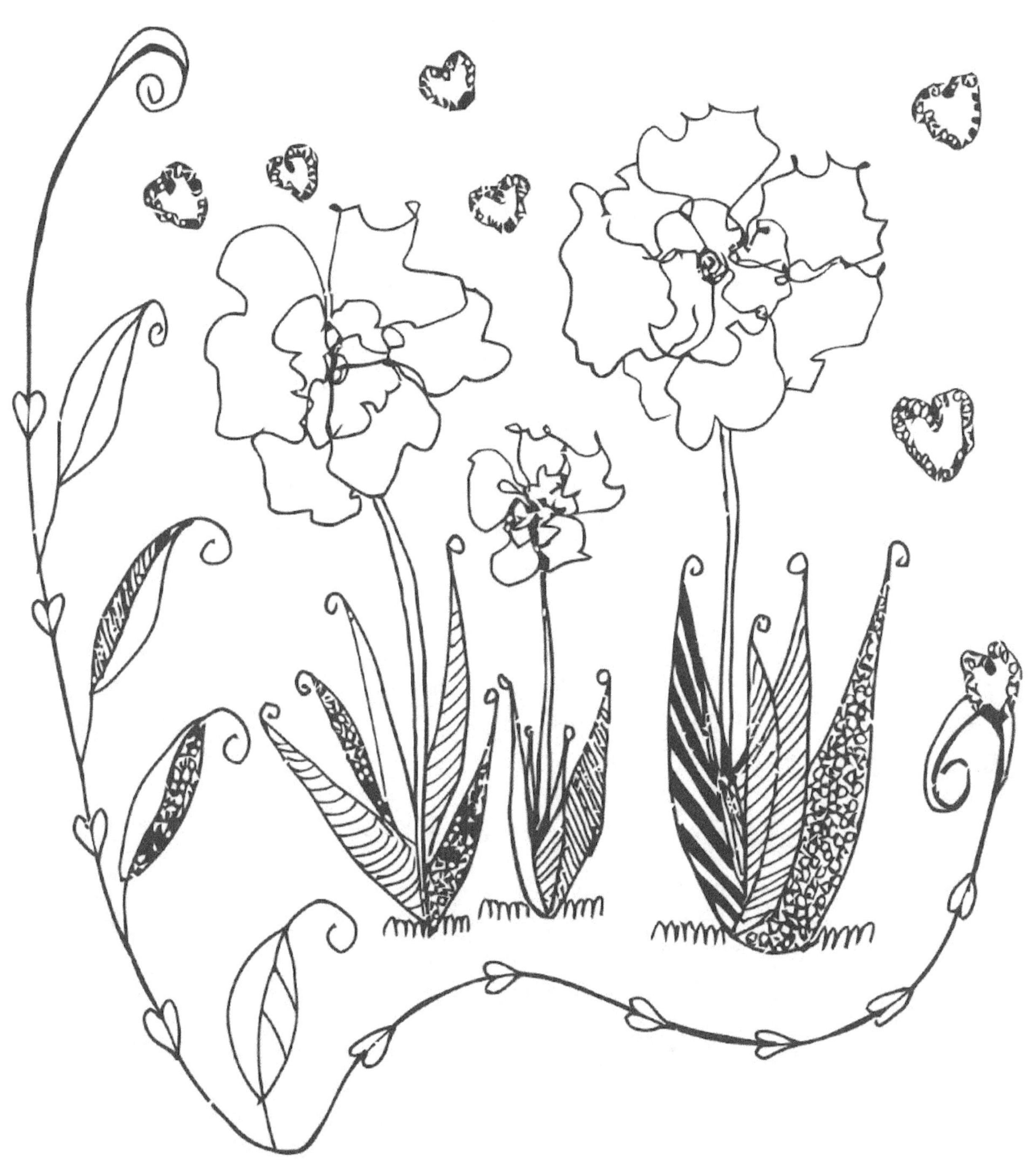

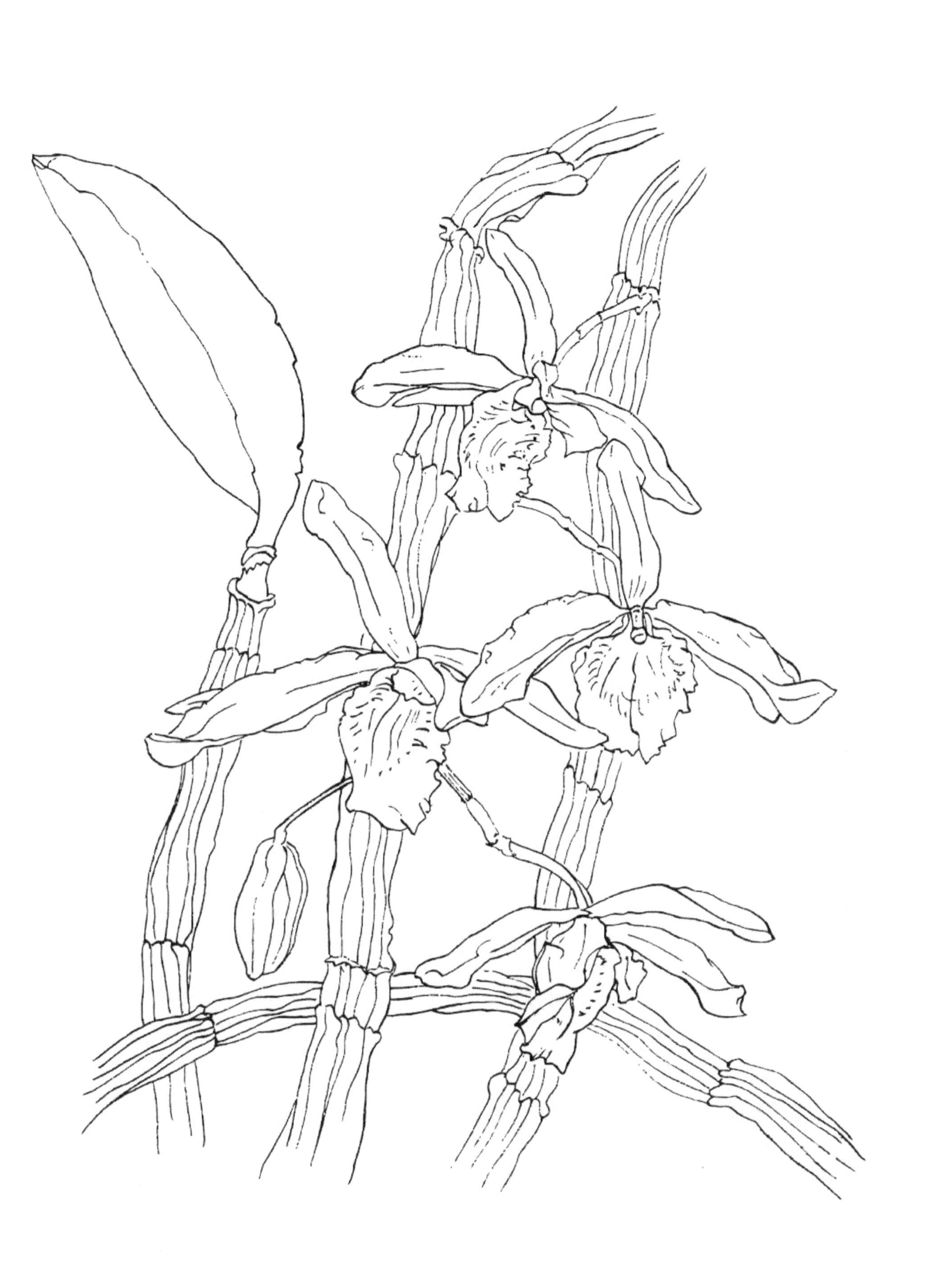

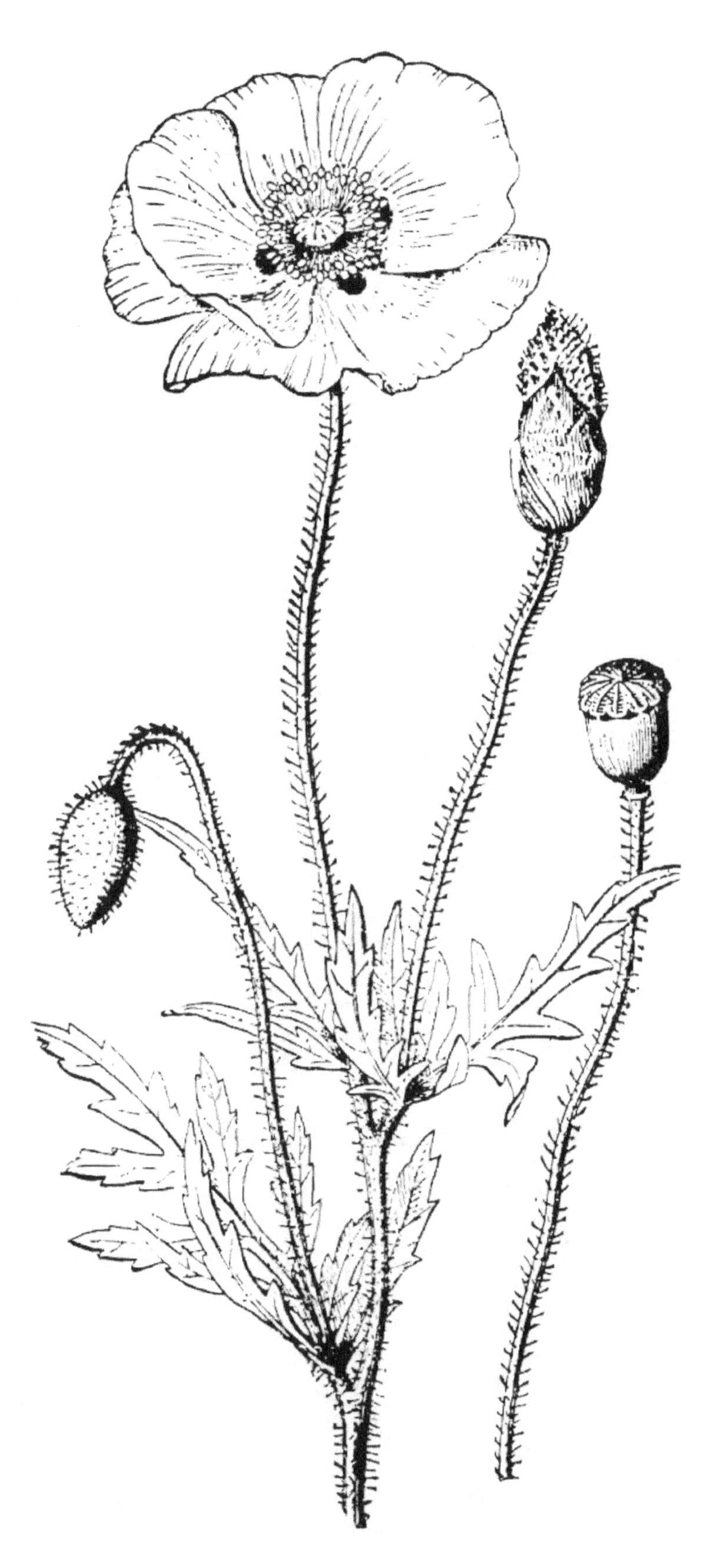

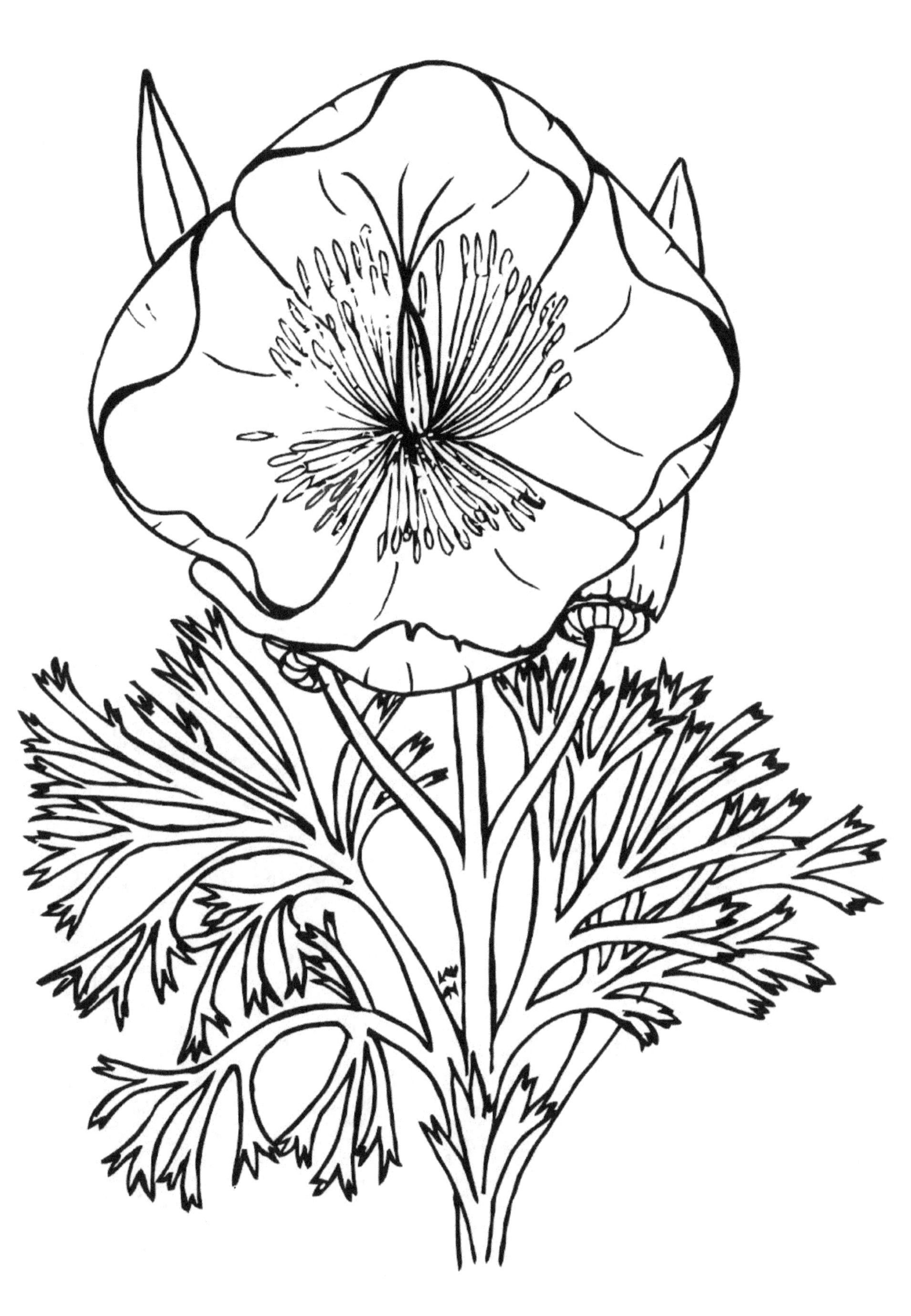

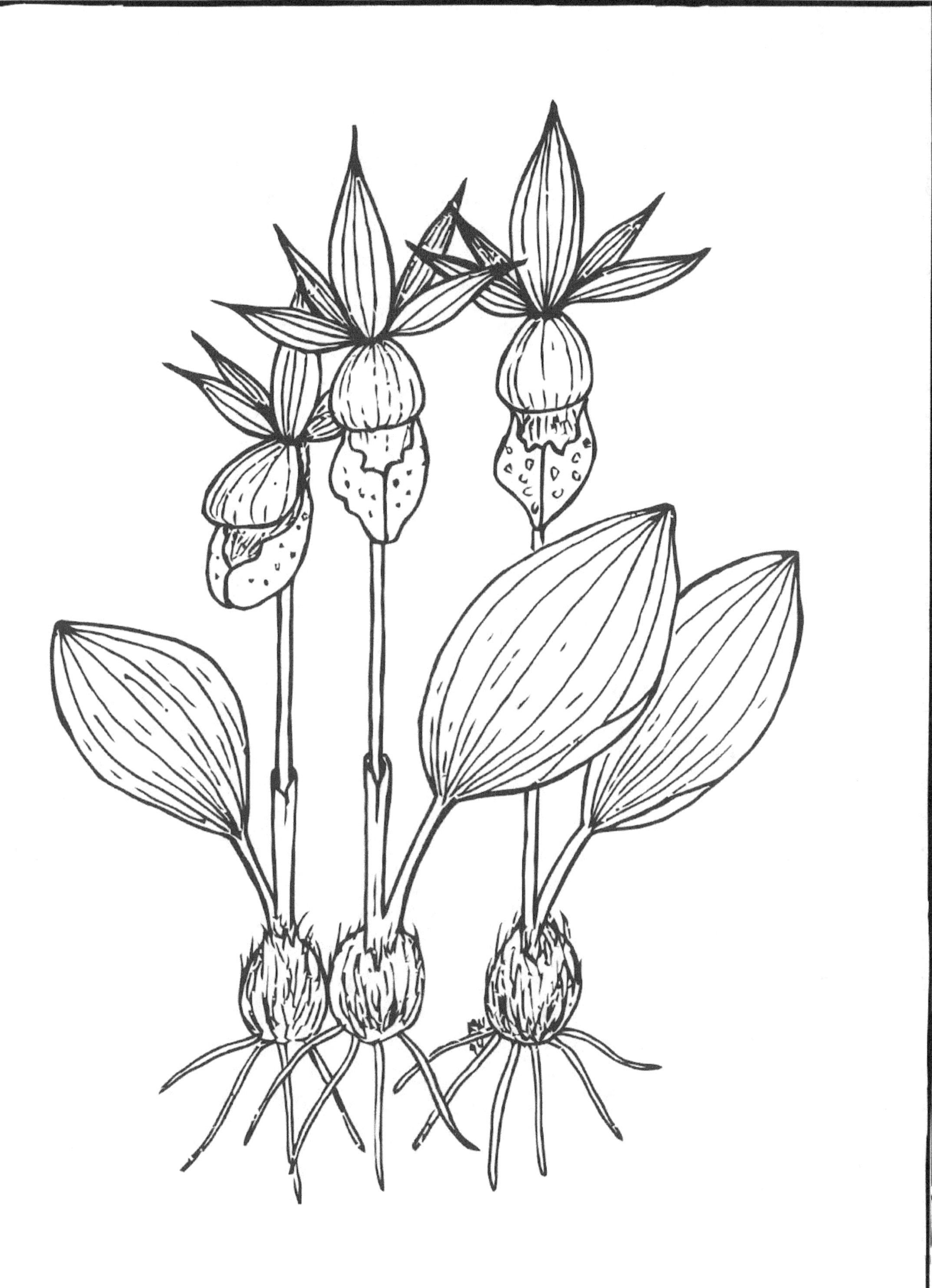

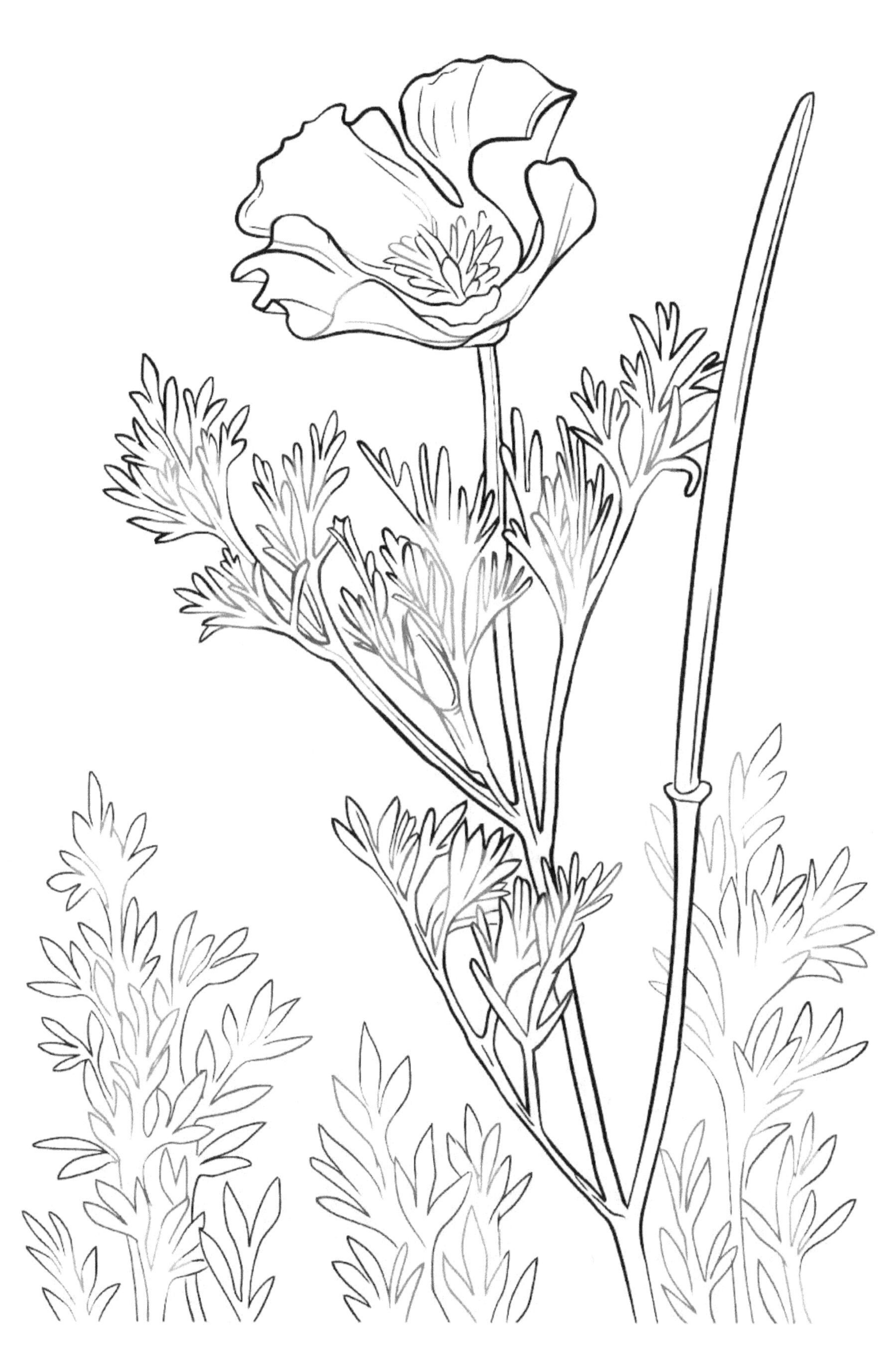

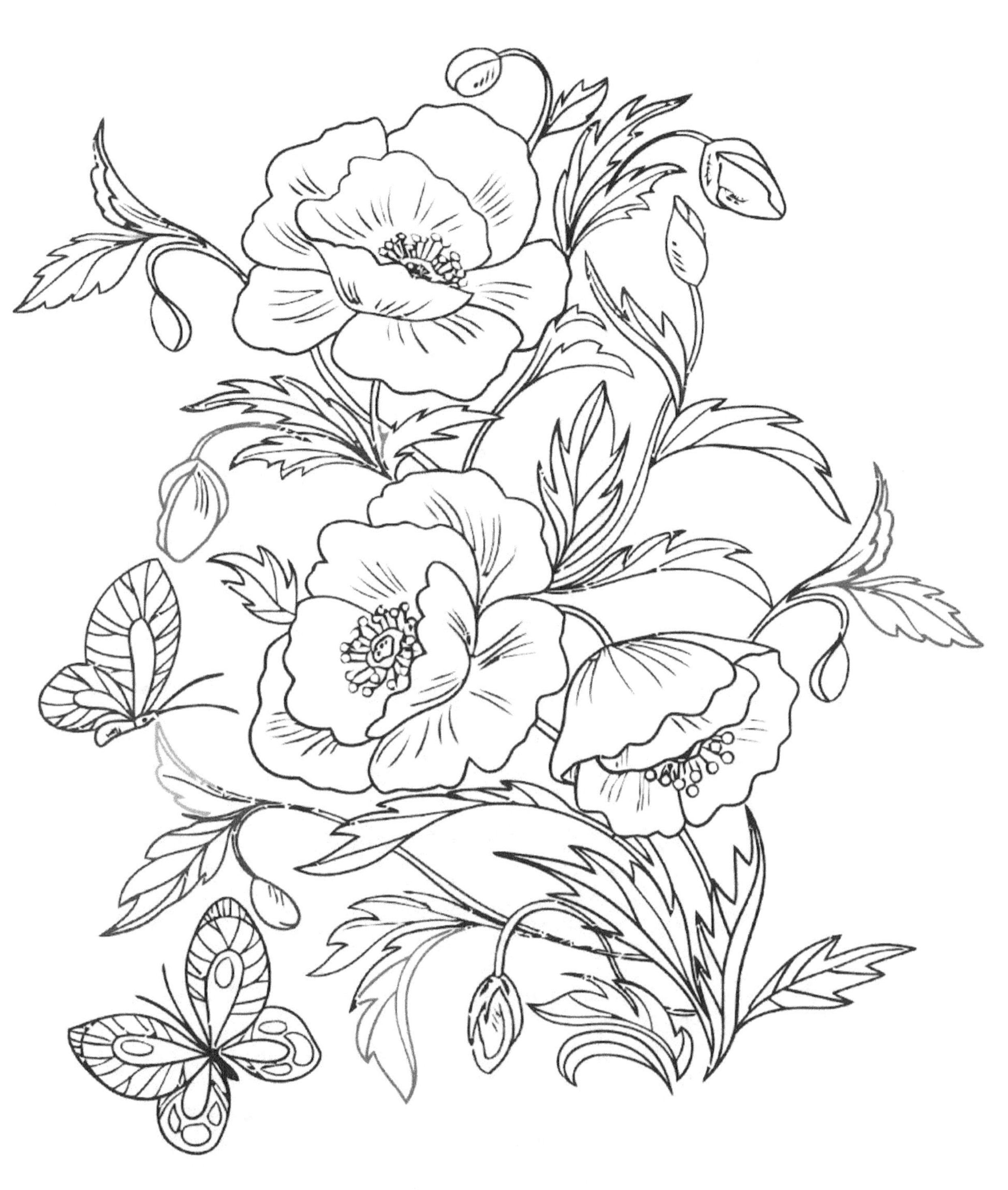

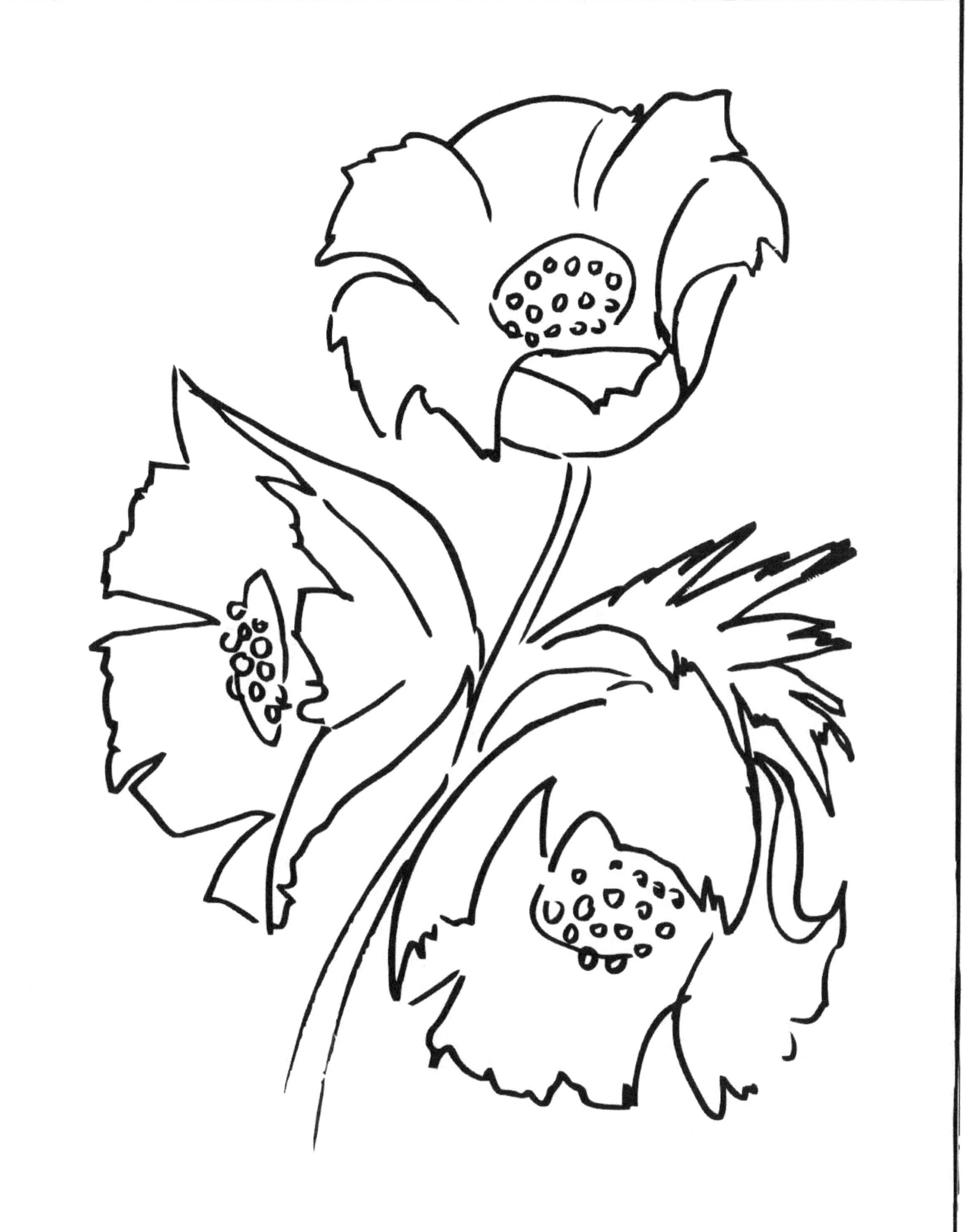

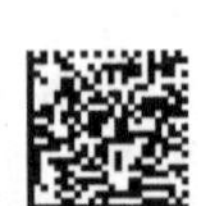

www.ingramcontent.com/pod-product-compliance
Lightning Source LLC
Chambersburg PA
CBHW081450250726
48662CB00009B/3012